The I-S

C000219371

CARS

MICHELIN

*(Title page) Sporting Jaguars for the second half of
the 1990s, the XJS in coupé and convertible forms.*

Note: No single volume – however wide-ranging – can include every
historic vehicle and every contemporary car. The subject is vast: new
models are coming out and being discontinued all the time, just as
they have for the last century. If a model which interests you is not
here, perhaps it will be included in the next edition.

© I-Spy Limited 1995

ISBN 1 85671 158 7

Michelin Tyre Public Company
Edward Hyde Building, 38 Clarendon Road,
Watford, Herts WD1 1SX

MICHELIN and the Michelin Man are Registered
Trademarks of Michelin

A CIP record for this title is available from the
British Library.

Edited by Neil Curtis. Designed by Richard Garratt .

Many of the photographs in this book have been
supplied by manufacturers, and the publisher is also
grateful to *Autocar* archives, Neill Bruce and the
Peter Roberts Collection, Richard Garatt, David
Hodges, Maurice Rowe, and Neil Curtis.
Compilation and captions by David Hodges.

Colour reproduction by Anglia Colour Ltd.

Printed in Spain by Graficromo SA.

INTRODUCTION

During the first century of motoring, perhaps three generations actually comprised a formative period, the approach to the independent personal transport we take for granted now. But we need to go back no more than forty years to a time when car journeys over long distances were seldom smooth, quick, or comfortable, when Continental motoring holidays were an adventure, and when many cars still conformed to a broad technical pattern established before World War II.

So we have divided this *I-Spy Guide to Cars* into two broad main sections, covering roughly the cars of the first three generations, and then cars that are widely encountered on today's roads. There is not a rigid divide, for part of the fascination of cars is the development story, sometimes on parallel lines, sometimes through periods of near stagnation, sometimes when a landmark model inspires an abrupt change of direction, as when the Mini showed beyond dispute that its layout was the right one for small cars. Incidentally, speed conversions are rounded, rather than precise.

The first section is largely chronologically arranged, the second essentially alphabetical, and the hundreds of models we illustrate and describe represent all categories of cars, from working vehicles that were built by the million to supercars. Then we have added a reminder of Grand Prix racing, for this is both a spectacle and a showcase for forms of advanced automotive engineering that might, just might, find a way on to production cars in the twenty-first century.

Daimler, 1886

Ancestor. The first self-propelled vehicles had steam engines but, in 1886, the German engineer, Gottlieb Daimler (1839–90), built his first four-wheel car with an internal combustion engine. It was a 'horseless carriage', with the shafts that ran alongside the horse removed, steering through four handles at the top of a column (a steering wheel was soon to come), and a single-cylinder 462 cc engine giving a nominal 1.1 bhp. The top speed was claimed to be 11 mph (18 kmh).

The First Generations

Rolls-Royce
The 40/50 'Silver Ghost' of 1907 is perhaps the most famous of all veteran cars. Here it is posed with a Rolls-Royce successor from some seventy years later, a 6.7-litre Camargue.

Benz Velo

The sturdy little Velo was the world's first series production car. It was introduced in 1894 and, in nine years, some 1200 were built. The Velo had a 1050 cc engine, rated at 1.5 bhp in 1894 and 3.5 bhp in 1902. Top speed was 12 mph (19 kmh).

Mercedes 60

Built in 1903–04, this was the production version of Wilhelm Maybach's Mercedes-Simplex design, advanced in aspects such as its pressed-steel chassis, and looking like a car rather than like a horseless carriage. Its 9.3-litre engine gave a top speed of 65 mph (105 kmh) but, like all early cars, there were no front wheel brakes.

De Dion Bouton

This two-seater is one of the most familiar of all veteran cars. It was practical and very popular in its day, when France briefly became the leading automotive nation. It was built from 1900 until 1913, always with single-cylinder engines (this 1903 car has a 700 cc unit). By modern standards, the engine compartment looks part empty.

Oldsmobile 'Curved Dash'

The American Ransom Eli Olds (1864–1950) built his first car in 1895, and the name of his company survived 100 years later. The 'Curved Dash' was his great success, an equivalent of the De Dion and built from 1901 until 1906, with production reaching 5000 in 1904. Its 1.5-litre single-cylinder engine lived under the seats. Like the De Dion, it could reach 20 mph (32 kmh).

Rolls-Royce 10 hp

British engineer Henry Royce (1863–1933) was not pleased by a Decauville he owned, so he built a better car. It impressed the Hon. C S Rolls (1877–1910) and, as a result, Rolls-Royce was set up. This 10 hp was the first 'production' model (only sixteen were built, 1904–06), and it introduced the classic radiator shape. It had a twin-cylinder, 10 bhp, engine. Passengers sat high and exposed.

Rover 16/20

Rover is another of the very few names from the pioneer years that still appears on cars, and the outline of the modern badge echoes the shape of the radiator introduced on the 20 hp model in 1907. It had a 3.1-litre, four-cylinder engine and was a solid, conventional vehicle, setting a pattern for most Rovers through the following decades.

Lanchester 38 hp

British car and aeronautics pioneer, Frederick Lanchester (1868–1946) designed high-class cars from first principles, but this 1913 38 hp 'Torpedo' was one of the last with its engine mounted well back, partly beside the driver. From 1914, his brother George designed Lanchesters with more orthodox layouts.

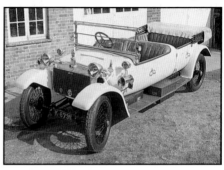

Renault AX

Renault has made light cars from its very first in 1898. The 1905–14 AX was the first with the 'coal scuttle' engine cover, named for its shape, with the radiator behind it. This 1909 AX was a cheap and reliable runabout. Its 1060 cc engine gave it a top speed of more than 30 mph (48 kmh).

Fiat Zero

Fiat's Tipo 1 from 1908, and this 1911–15 Zero, established the small-to-medium ranges usually associated with the Italian company. The Zero had a 1.8-litre engine and four-speed gearbox, and could reach 50 mph (80 kmh). Most had four-seater bodies, while specialists built two-seaters like this one at the National Motor Museum.

Ford Model T

Between 1908 and 1927, more than 15 million Ts were sold – a record that lasted until the 1970s. It was mechanically simple, with a 2.9-litre engine giving a top speed of only 42 mph (68 kmh), but it provided reliable basic transport for countless new motorists. American-built Ts were black because that was the only quick-drying paint available at the time, called for by Henry Ford's mass production methods. Ts were built in Britain from 1911.

Mercer Type 35

An American forerunner of the sports car, the T35 Raceabout was a conservative design, built to high standards for wealthy sporting motorists. Bodywork was simple, with only a little 'monocle' windscreen to protect the driver, and there was an exposed fuel tank. This 5-litre car could reach 70 mph (115 kmh). It dates from 1911.

Vauxhall Prince Henry

Big four-seat tourers were also ancestors of sports cars. The Prince Henry was named for its success in a German long-distance trial – an early rally – in 1910. This 1911 production version had a fast-revving 3-litre engine; a 4-litre model with better performance came a year later.

Hispano-Suiza Alphonso

This Franco-Spanish company named its Type 15T for King Alphonso XIII of Spain, a keen motorist. It was an advanced car, built with a variety of two- and four-seat bodies. All were sporting models, with 3.6-litre engines giving lively performance and top speeds approaching 80 mph (130 kmh).

Rolls-Royce 40/50

Produced in chassis form 1906–25, the 40/50 carried bodies by specialist coachbuilders, from open tourers, such as the Silver Ghost, to this dignified 1914 landau (the roof behind the rear doors could be lowered). 'Ghost' became an unofficial name. The 40/50 had a 7-litre straight six, and although it was improved, front-wheel brakes were not fitted until 1924.

Citroën 'C'

As the 1920s opened, inexpensive 'real' small cars displaced the primitive cyclecars, with Citroën's 'C' setting an example, in the tradition of the little De Dion shown on page 7. The 'C' was easy to drive and maintain, while an 11 bhp engine gave adequate performance. Like this 1921 car, early 'Cs' were yellow, and were dubbed 'Citron'.

Morris Cowley

The Bullnose Morris first appeared in 1913, but the Cowley and Oxford of the 1920s are usually associated with the nickname. This is a 1922 two-seat Cowley, which was slightly less powerful than the Oxford, with a 26 bhp 1.5-litre engine. The artillery wheels are typical of the period.

Trojan 10 hp

Trojan's contributions to the spread of popular motoring in the 1920s were basic models such as this 10 hp car of 1925 which had a two-stroke engine under the floor (despite a conventional bonnet), chain drive, and solid tyres. This 1.5-litre 10 hp was the cheapest car on the British market, costing £125.

Austin Seven

Sir Herbert Austin's Seven was hurried into production in 1923, and it became a motoring legend – versions were later to be built in Japan and the United States, and by BMW and Rosengart in Germany and France. It was very light, its 747 cc engine was rated at 10.5 bhp, and its brakes were feeble. This is a 1930 Chummy.

Morris Minor

The Minor was William Morris's response to the 'Baby Austin'. It was a little larger, and better equipped, with an 847 cc engine giving a top speed of 55 mph (88 kmh). Between 1929 and 1934 up to a dozen body styles were offered – this tourer is typical – but sales failed to match those of the Austin Seven. The name was used for later small Morris models.

Lancia Lambda

Vincenzo Lancia's master-piece had the world's first unitary chassis/body construction, an unusual V4 engine, independent front suspension to contribute to good road holding and handling, and excellent four-wheel brakes. It looked dull, but was an outstanding touring or sporting car. The last cars, built through to 1931, had platform chassis so that specialist coach-builders could fit bodies.

Napier 40/50

Napier made great efforts to rival Rolls-Royce with this carefully engineered luxury car. Its weight gave it a solid feel, while its ohc, six-cylinder, 6.2-litre engine gave a top speed of about 70 mph (115 km h) – faster than Rolls's 40/50. This rare survivor has a cabriolet, or soft-top, body. Sales were disappointing, and Napier car production ended in 1924.

Bentley 3-litre

The rough roads and race circuits of the 1920s meant that sports cars had to be big and tough, and Bentley proved the point at Le Mans. Two of its victories in the classic 24-hour race were scored with 3-litre cars. This Speed Model, built in 1925, was one of more than 500; it had an 85 bhp engine and a top speed of 80 mph (130 kmh).

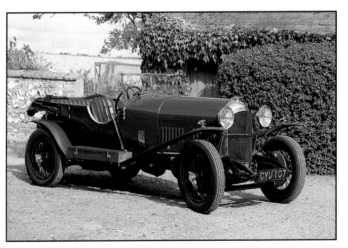

Bentley Speed Six

W O Bentley preferred big, lightly stressed engines. When his 6½-litre power unit was introduced in 1925, it was intended for heavy saloon cars. The sports version, the Speed Six, came two-and-a-half years later and twice won at Le Mans. This car has a well-proportioned drophead coupé body by the famous coachbuilder, Mulliner.

Bugatti Royale

Ettore Bugatti designed his Type 41 on a grand scale, but no Royales were sold to royal families. Some of the six actually built have been rebodied more than once. These flamboyant and overvalued cars were at least 6.7 metres (22 ft) long and had 12.7-litre engines – these found a use in railcars when the Type 41 was a sales flop.

Rolls-Royce 20/25

This was the small R-R of the 1930s, developed from the Twenty, with its engine enlarged from 3.1 to 3.7 litres. Some 3800 were built between 1929 and 1937, and supplied in chassis form to specialist coachbuilders. Many of their bodies, such as this 1932 sports saloon by Park Ward, were slightly old-fashioned.

Packard 160

Through the 1930s, American manufacturers produced some of the finest luxury cars, rivalling the best in Europe. This 7.7-litre V12-engined town car in Packard's 'Senior Series' has a coachbuilt body by Brunn which complemented the smooth multi-cylinder engine.

Auburn Speedster

The Model 851 Speedster was a flamboyant two-seater, the nearest thing to a sports car built in America in the 1930s, and a Hollywood favourite. Despite the overall size of the car, there was little room in the cockpit. Its 4.6-litre straight eight was usually in supercharged form, and the claimed 100 mph (160 kmh) top speed was proved in predelivery tests.

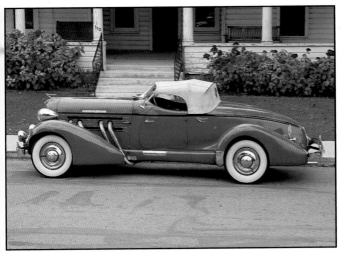

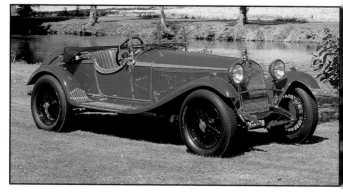

Alfa Romeo 6C

The lithe Zagato body identifies this as one of the series of six- and eight-cylinder Alfa Romeos that set new sports car standards in the late 1920s and early '30s, on roads or tracks. This is a 1.7-litre 6C – an 85 bhp, 100 mph (160 kmh) classic.

MG PA

Although MG built saloons and large sports cars, it was usually identified with small cars in the 1930s. These had engines derived from the Morris Minor unit. The cars looked skimpy, had stiff suspension, and a ride that was hardly comfortable, but they were fun! This 1935 PA, with an Airline body, shows that fastback styles are not new. With an 847 cc 35 bhp engine, it had a top speed approaching 75 mph (120 kmh).

MG TA Midget

First of the cherished T-Series Midgets came in 1936, and the 1.3-litre TA was continued until 1939. Handling was good, the ride was better than earlier Midgets – although still far from smooth – and the 52 bhp engine gave it a top speed of 80 mph (130 kmh).

Frazer Nash TT Replica

There were still distinctive cars in the 1930s. The 'chain gang' Frazer Nash stands out for its chain final drive, with separate clutch and chain for each speed. This made for light and quick gear changes, ideal for cars such as this 1937, 1.5-litre, 80 mph+ (130 kmh) TT Replica.

Armstrong Siddeley 20

This British company built some sporting cars but was noted for its high-quality saloons, which were comfortable rather than stylish. They were also easy to drive because of the Wilson preselector gearbox – not a full automatic 'box in the modern sense, but a system that did not require a clutch pedal. This is a 1935 Burlington saloon.

Bugatti Type 57

T57s are among the most familiar Bugattis, with sleek bodies clothing mechanical elements that were becoming dated when the model was introduced in 1934. This is a 1937 coupé. Cars with the normal 3.3-litre straight eight reached 95 mph (153 kmh) and the supercharged T57C was good for 110 mph (177 kmh).

Delahaye 135M

The 135, in saloon and sports forms, revived the fortunes of this French company in the 1930s. Introduced in 1935, the 3.2-litre engine had its origins in a truck power unit. Refined saloons, such as this 1938 135M, were comfortable and could reach about 90 mph (145 kmh).

Riley 9 Monaco

All Riley 9s were highly rated as 'drivers' cars' in their day. The saloons were named Monaco, Falcon, or Kestrel. This 1934 Monaco bridged the gap between a fabric-bodied version and a sleek 1936 car. All 9s had efficient 1.1-litre overhead-valve engines.

Austin 10

The Austin 10/4 was run from 1932, revised with these more modern lines for 1934, then revised again for 1937–39. Several body styles were listed, the saloons having names such as Lichfield and Cambridge. A 1.1-litre engine gave these Austin family cars top speeds of about 55 mph (90 kmh).

Ford Model Y

The Y was the first European Ford (rather than a transplanted US model) and, in its economy form, it became Britain's first £100 car, in 1935. It was built with 'Tudor' (two-door) and 'Fordor' (four-door) saloon bodies, 1932–37. Its 23 bhp 733 cc engine (an '8' for tax purposes) would have propelled this 1936 8Y to almost 60 mph (95 kmh).

Jaguar SS100

Strictly this car was an SS ('Swallow Sidecars'), but Jaguar was added to the initials in 1936. It was introduced as a 2½-litre sports car, and the 3½-litre version shown came in 1938. In that form, the SS100 handsomely exceeded 100 mph (160 kmh). Its low sleek lines were sensational in the 1930s. These SS Jaguars became better known as rally cars than for racing.

BMW 328

Like the SS100, this BMW set new sports car standards in the late 1930s, and its body lines were to inspire later designs. It had a clever adaptation of an earlier 2-litre engine and, in standard form, it could just reach 100 mph (160 kmh). A version of this engine was used in the first Bristol cars. Between 1936 and 1939, BMW's production of the classic 328 was a mere 462 cars.

Ferrari 125

Enzo Ferrari's (1898–1988) first car had the Auto-Avio badge, and the first to carry his name was the 125, built in 1947. In 1988 the company went back to the original drawings to construct this replica of that historic 125; it is faithful to the original in every respect. With a 1.5-litre V12, that car could reach 100 mph (160 kmh).

Rover Twelve

This typical late-1930s design was revived after World War II, and normally built in saloon form – the four-seat open tourer was built only in 1947. The 1.5-litre engine did not give an exciting performance but, for the period, this was a pleasant car, and it is now a rare one.

Jowett Javelin

This was a surprising car to come from Jowett, notable for its unadventurous models in the 1930s. Javelin was an advanced design, with a new engine, sound aerodynamics, and a 'wheel at each corner' for good road holding. Its 1.5-litre engine propelled it to 80 mph (130 kmh), and it was roomy and comfortable. It was built from 1947 until 1953, when the company had to stop making cars.

Morris Minor

The curves of the body mark this out as a car of the late 1940s. In 1948 it was all new, apart from its 918 cc engine, which meant that early Minors – distinguished by low-set headlights – struggled to 60 mph (95 kmh). Later versions had more power: 803 cc engines from 1952, then 948 cc from 1956, and 1098 cc from 1962, to give a speed approaching 80 mph (128 kmh). Minors were listed in saloon, tourer, estate car, van and pick-up forms; more than 1.6 million were built before production ended in 1972.

Citroën 2CV

Names like 'garden shed on wheels' were affectionate, and the 2CV sold more than twice as well as the Minor. Introduced in 1948, it was made in England as well as in France during 1954–59; French production ended in 1988, and the last 2CVs were built in Portugal in 1990. It was a simple go-anywhere utility vehicle. Early versions with 375 cc air-cooled engines managed about 40 mph (65 kmh); the 425 cc versions from 1954 were a little faster, and finally, there was a 602 cc 2CV which, with a good following wind, could achieve 70 mph (110 kmh).

Renault 4CV

In the late 1940s and through the '50s, the 'rear-engined' layout seemed best for small cars, despite the limitations this imposed on luggage space and the poor handling qualities that sometimes resulted from weight distribution and suspension compromises. Renault's 4CV (1947–61) could carry four people in reasonable comfort but, with a 750 cc engine, was pushed to reach 60 mph (100 kmh). More than a million were sold.

Renault Dauphine

Introduced in 1956, effectively as an updated and roomier 4CV, the Dauphine had an 845 cc engine to give a top speed approaching 70 mph (112 kmh). Its lines were attractive, but the bodywork was notoriously rust-prone. It was the first French car to sell more than two million.

Volkswagen Beetle

The Beetle was laid out in the late 1930s, but true production did not start until 1945. It became legendary, and the world's best-selling car – although European production ended in 1977, it continued in Brazil and Mexico into the 1990s. The divided rear window shows this is an early car. The Beetle was progressively improved, and its air-cooled engine enlarged, but it always provided basic individual transport.

SEAT 133

Small Fiats were also rear engined through this period, and the Italian company's models had long lives, and sometimes second lives – this is a SEAT, a version of the 850 which Fiat built 1964–72 that was made in Spain. The 843 cc engine gave up to 75 mph (120 kmh), and this rear-engined car had good handling.

Triumph Renown

Under Standard company control, Triumph introduced 'razor-edge' angular styling on the 1800 and 2000 from 1946, and this type of body was combined with Standard Vanguard chassis and suspension in the 2.1-litre Renown, 1949–54. Room and visibility were claimed advantages of this style.

Museums

Around twenty-five British museums are devoted to road transport, while some national or regional museums, such as the Science Museum, the Glasgow Museum of Transport, the Birmingham Museum of Transport and Industry, and the Bristol Industrial Museum, have substantial road vehicle interests. Related forms of transport can be studied at dedicated collections, from the National Tramway Museum at Crich to the National Motorcycle Museum near Solihull. Other important collections are within easy reach nowadays; for example, Autoworld at Brussels, the French National Motor Museum at Mulhouse, or the early vehicles in the basement of the chateau at Compiegne; while manufacturers, such as Alfa Romeo, BMW, Mercedes-Benz, and Peugeot maintain impressive collections.

Major British car collections can be found at:

The Brooklands Museum, Weybridge, Surrey – Tel. (01932) 857381;

The Donington Collection, Castle Donington, Derby – Tel. (01332) 810048;

Haynes Motor Museum, Sparkford, Somerset – Tel. (01963) 40804;

Heritage Motor Centre, Gaydon, Warwick – Tel. (01926) 641188;

Midlands Motor Museum, Bridgnorth, Shropshire – Tel. (01746) 761761;

Museum of British Road Transport, Coventry – Tel. (01203) 832425;

National Motor Museum, Beaulieu, Hants – Tel. (01590) 612345;

Totnes Motor Museum, Totnes, Devon – Tel. (01803) 862777;

The Yorkshire Car Collection, Keighley, West Yorks – Tel. (01535) 690499.

Bristol 400

The Bristol Aeroplane Company started building cars in 1947, with this high-performance luxury saloon – later it might have been called a GT car. Mechanical components had BMW origins, notably a version of the late-1930s 2-litre engine. Smooth aerodynamic body lines, developed in a wind tunnel, helped the 400 exceed 90 mph (145 kmh). It was listed until 1950, with just 474 built.

Daimler Conquest

This was one of the models that marked Daimler's move from a wide traditional range towards cars that were still well equipped but had a sporting bias. It was built 1953–56, joined in 1954 by the Conquest Century which had a developed version of the 2.4-litre engine giving it a 90 mph (145 kmh) top speed.

Jaguar XK120

Sensational when it was exhibited before full production started in 1949, and still eye-catching, this first two-seater in Jaguar's XK series was powered by a twin-cam straight six engine that was still being built four decades later. In 3.4-litre form in the XK120, it was first rated at 160 bhp, and that gave the car a top speed of more than 120 mph (190 kmh). The car illustrated was successful in major rallies in the 1950s.

AC Ace

A combination of a chassis/suspension design by John Tojeiro, a body that was inspired by Ferrari's barchetta style, and an engine that had its origins in 1919 made up this successful British sports car (1954–63). Power was an inadequate 80 bhp at first, then a 2-litre 125 bhp Bristol engine gave the Ace a 117 mph (187 kmh) maximum speed.

Classic Car Shows

Dedicated classic car exhibitions under cover are topped by two at the National Exhibition Centre at Birmingham, held in the late spring and early winter. These include many club and trade stands, 'special features' as rare models are shown off in centre pieces, and restoration activities. Autojumble areas at these shows, and others, reflect a fascinating flea-market aspect to the classic car hobby; others are found out of doors at more favourable times of year, with an enormous one in the National Motor Museum grounds in September.

Exhibitions principally dedicated to modern cars, such as the Racing Car Show at the beginning of the year, often have interest sections, while classic car auctions are held at the London Motor Show, with the entries on view in the days before the auction (admission to many other auctions is by catalogue only).

MG TD

Obviously in a line of evolution from the late 1930s, the TD was built 1950–53, and most were left-hand drive cars for the US market. Compared with the TC, its improvements were at the front, in suspension and steering, and agility made up for a disappointing top speed of 80 mph (130 kmh) with the normal 57 bhp engine. The MkII (illustrated) had a little more power.

Triumph TR2

The TR2 was another simple and practical sports car. It was cheap, had mediocre handling, and spartan equipment. Using the Standard Vanguard engine in 90 bhp form, it had a 108 mph (173 kmh) top speed. It was the first production model in the TR line, and 8628 were built (1953–55) before it gave way to TR3.

Chrysler 300C

The mid-1950s was a period of excess chrome and fins in American fashion, here shown in Chrysler's 'Flite Sweep' styling. A 6.4-litre, 395 bhp, V8 gave the 300C of 1957 the power to compete with Ford's Thunderbird. Fewer than 2000 of these coupés were made.

Chevrolet Corvette

The Corvette was Chevrolet's idea of an American sports car for the 1950s, and the General Motors company was still using the name more than forty years later. The first 1953–54 'Vette had a straight six rated at only 150 bhp, giving a 107 mph (172 kmh) maximum speed, and it

had a two-speed automatic transmission. Yet it was developed into a sports car. The use of glass-fibre bodywork was a brave innovation.

Ford Mustang

Ford introduced the Mustang in the United States as a 'personal car', rather than as a sports car, in 1964. There was a platform chassis and options of straight six or V8 engines in the first cars, the latter giving up to 210 bhp in the 4.7-litre form. Soon a lot of work was put into tuning these very successful four-seaters, and Carroll Shelby was to develop a real sports car version.

Aston Martin DB2/4

David Brown took over Aston Martin in 1947 – hence DB. The DB1 was modified to accept a straight six designed by W O Bentley for the associated Lagonda company, and this model was designated DB2. The DB2/4 (illustrated) came in 1953, with a 2.6-litre engine, and was a flexible 110 mph (175 kmh) car with excellent road manners. Later DB2/4s had 2.9-litre engines and slightly longer bodies.

Bentley R Type Continental

This car set Bentley apart from contemporary Rolls-Royce models, which shared components. It was the fastest four-seater available in 1952, capable of speeds approaching 120 mph (190 kmh). The chassis was the normal R Type, but it carried superb light alloy fastback bodywork by H J Mulliner. Only 207 were built, early ones with 4.6-litre engines, late ones with 4.9 litres; either is now a rare classic.

Citroën 11

The first of André Citroën's *tractions* – front-wheel drive models – came in 1934, and development costs forced the company into bankruptcy, when it was saved by Michelin. That 7CV also pioneered the mass production of a unitary construction car. The 11CV (illustrated) came in 1935 and was continued into the 1950s. The normal version was built in Britain as well as in France, unlike the large 7-9 seater with the same 1.9-litre engine.

Citroën 15/6

The big *traction* with a 2.9-litre six-cylinder engine was introduced in 1939 (when a few were made in Britain, in a de-luxe form). With a top speed capability of more than 80 mph (130 kmh), it was some 10 mph faster than the 11. Late cars, in 1954–55, had hydro-pneumatic rear suspension.

Mini

Introduced late in 1959 with Austin or Morris badges, Alec Issigonis's Mini design set new small-car standards, and was the inspiration for many later models. Front-wheel drive was combined with a transverse 848 cc engine, to 'package' mechanical components and passenger space within a short wheelbase. Developments followed through to the 1990s.

Citroën Ami

In some ways, the Ami was a 'grown-up' 2CV, without that car's charm. More space and power were offered in the 1961–69 Ami 6, with a 602 cc twin-cylinder engine (that gave 60 mph/100 kmh potential). There was still more power in the 1968–78 Ami 8, and a four-cylinder 1015 cc engine in the 1973–76 Super.

Panhard 24CT

During the 1960s, front-wheel drive became widely accepted for small and medium cars. At the time, the ancient Panhard company was fading and its last model was the distinctive 24CT. This had outstanding performance with a twin-cylinder 845 cc engine – with this in the 60 bhp Tigre form, it was capable of almost 100 mph (160 kmh).

Renault 4

Renault turned to front-wheel drive in the 3 (an underpowered car sold mainly in France) and the 4, a practical competitor for Citroën's 2CV – more than 8 million were sold from its 1961 introduction until production ended in Argentina in 1991. The 4 had twin-cylinder engines of 603 cc and 747 cc, and 848 cc for most markets, and finally an 1108 cc four-cylinder unit that propelled it to 82 mph (131 kmh).

Jaguar Mk II

Jaguar's highly successful line of compact saloons was introduced with the 2.4 in 1955. The Mk II, from 1959, had a closely similar body and 2.4-, 3.4-, and 3.8-litre versions of the famous straight six. The largest was rated at 220 bhp, and the 3.8 could reach 126 mph (203 kmh).

Volvo P1800

The first production examples of this attractive sporting coupé were built in Britain by Jensen for the Swedish company. Both P1800 (1961–63, with a 1.8-litre engine) and P1800S (1963–69, with 2 litres) were solid cars, comfortable for two people. The P1800S could achieve 115 mph (185 kmh).

Porsche 356

The 356 designation was first used by Porsche in 1949, for two-seaters based on the VW Beetle. Variants appeared through to 1965, with this 356B built in 1959–63. There were four body styles, with rear-mounted air-cooled 1.6-litre engines in 60, 75, and 90 bhp forms. All gave top speeds of more than 100 mph (160 kmh).

Triumph Herald

Production expediency meant that this small, four-seat, two-door saloon was unusual when it was introduced in 1959, for its separate chassis and all-independent suspension. The first version had a 948 cc engine, but the 1200 from the mid-1960s had 1147 cc and reached 75 mph (120 kmh). There were also convertible and estate car versions.

Hillman Imp

If this rear-engined small car had come before the Mini, it would have been a great success. An efficient 875 cc engine gave 77 mph (123 kmh) in the first Imps, but the model suffered many teething problems and gained a reputation for handling shortcomings on wet roads. More than 440,000 were built, 1963–76.

Fiat 500

Fiat's 'baby car' theme was carried through the 1960s and on to 1975 by this rear-engined car, while a station wagon version lasted until 1977. An air-cooled twin-cylinder engine pushed it to about 60 mph (95 kmh). Noisy and cramped, it was a useful runabout, and some 3 million were built.

Alvis TD21

The last Alvis cars had very attractive bodies styled by Graber, and TC to TF were built in small numbers 1956–63. This TD21, introduced in 1958, was the only model to achieve a four-figure production (1070); like the others, it had a 3-litre six-cylinder engine. Its top speed was 105 mph (169 kmh).

Armstrong Siddeley Star Sapphire

The last of the Sapphire line, dating from 1952, the 1958–60 Star Sapphire was highly rated, but it was also Armstrong Siddeley's last car. It followed in the tradition of building luxury saloons with a high performance, in this case a maximum speed of just over 100 mph (160 kmh).

Classics in Action

Cars of the past can be seen running at events from local carnivals and fêtes to gatherings of marque or even one-model enthusiasts, and major international festivals, from spring to autumn. One outstanding event takes place as winter is about to set in – the London-Brighton run, for Veteran Cars built before the end of 1904.

The RAC also organizes a vast early summer gathering, when hundreds of cars, from starting points as varied as Brooklands and Dublin, converge on Silverstone in the Norwich Union Classic. More serious rallying for not-so-old
cars takes place in the Rally Britannia, run at the time of the RAC Rally late in the year. There are many one-make club rallies, often in conjunction with meets.

Two major events on every enthusiast's calendar are the Goodwood Festival of Speed and the International Historic Festival at

Mercedes-Benz 300SL

The famous Gullwing coupé of the mid-1950s was named for its roof-hinged doors – conventional doors would have jeopardized the strength of the space frame. The 3-litre straight six was inclined, so that bonnet height could be low. It gave 240 bhp and 140 mph (225 kmh), but handling peculiarities with a swing-axle rear suspension made it a car for expert drivers only.

Austin-Healey 3000

These big muscular sports cars gained a great reputation in rallies. The first came in 1959, Mk II was built 1961–63, and Mk III (illustrated) until 1968 – 41,534 were built. All had a 2.9-litre straight six, rated at 148 bhp in the Mk III. That was a 120 mph (193 kmh) car.

Silverstone. Both feature racing cars – and others – in action, and both attract rare machines among the hundreds of entries. The space and permanent facilities at Silverstone mean that many car clubs can have their own gatherings within the two-day event.

Facel Vega HK500

Jean Daninos made a brave effort to maintain the traditional French Grand Routier in the 1950s and '60s, although he had to fall back on big Chrysler V8s to power most of his cars. The HK500 typified these when introduced as a sporting coupé in 1957; 500 were built before it gave way to Facel II, the last big Facel Vega, in 1961.

Maserati 3500

The famous Italian constructor turned to the luxury GT category with this 1957–64 model. Most of the 2200 plus that were built were coupés with bodies by Touring or convertibles with bodies by Vignale. Power came from a 3.5-litre straight six, which gave a top speed around 145 mph (235 kmh).

Lamborghini 350GT

This was Ferruccio Lamborghini's first production car, as he challenged Ferrari in the supercar market. The heart of the car was a magnificent 3.5-litre V12, which gave a top speed of 150 mph (240 kmh). The coupé body was styled by Touring. Only 131 were built in 1964–67 before Lamborghini turned to the 400GT.

Ferrari 250GT0

This most sought-after Ferrari has attracted astronomical values when one of the thirty-nine built (1962–64) has appeared at auction. It usually had a 3-litre V12 and could reach 175 mph (280 kmh). The finest car in Ferrari's first large-scale production 250GT series, it was suitable for road use or racing.

Jaguar E-type

Still regarded by many as the most beautiful Jaguar sports car (and rare because of rust problems), this first E was built 1961–64. It had a 3.8-litre version of Jaguar's immortal straight six engine, and a maximum speed of 145 mph (234 kmh). A 4.2-litre engine came in 1965; then the V12 that called for a larger air intake, spoiling the nose lines, came with the Series 3 cars for 1971.

Austin A30

Austin's first unitary construction model, announced in 1951 with an 803 cc engine. Late in 1956, the A35 followed, with the BMC A-series 948 cc engine giving a top speed of 72 mph (115 kmh), some 8 mph faster than the A30.

Austin-Healey Sprite

This small sports two-seater got its 'Frogeye' nickname from the appearance of the headlights. The engine from the A35 gave it modest performance – it just reached 80 mph (130 kmh). Despite this, it has great appeal for enthusiasts, and not just in Britain – most sales of a faithful replica built in the 1990s were to Japan. In 1964 the original gave way to the Sprite II.

MG Midget

An old MG name was revived for this car, which shared its body with the Sprite II. Early cars also had the 948 cc engine; Mk II and Mk III (illustrated) were more refined, with a 1275 cc engine giving 65 bhp and 85 mph (135 kmh). The Mk IV was run 1969–74. All were fun cars, in the Midget tradition.

Lotus Elan

Most of Colin Chapman's Lotus cars were as sophisticated as the MGs were simple. The Elan came in 1962, with a backbone chassis, all-independent suspension, and a glass-fibre body. All-round performance was outstanding.

The Elan Sprint (illustrated) appeared in 1971, with a 1.6-litre engine giving a top speed of over 120 mph (193 kmh). The Elan +2 had a longer wheelbase, to allow for two small rear seats. Elan production ended in 1974.

Citroën DS19

Revolutionary middle-class car when announced in 1955, and in many respects still a class leader through the 1960s, the DS had front-wheel drive, self-levelling hydropneumatic suspension, power-assisted gear-change, clutch, and brakes, and good aerodynamics – let down to a degree by an engine designed about twenty years earlier. Early cars – this is one of the first – could achieve only 87 mph (140 kmh).

Saab 96

Through to the 1970s, ral█ cars were less specialize█ than their modern counte█ parts, sometimes wi█ 'preparation' extending n█ further than the addition o█ accessories. Saab's 96 wa█ a surprisingly successf█ international rally car, for █ seemed underpowered wit█ an air-cooled, three█ cylinder, two-stroke engin█ of only 841 cc. This drov█ through the front wheels█ The aerodynamic line█ showed that Saab was fir█ and foremost an aircra█ manufacturer.

Mini Cooper

In its Cooper form, especially the S shown on a Monte Carlo Rally, the Mini was a great rally car, with victories in the classic winter event in 1965 and 1967 to its credit. It was also a spectacular and successful circuit racing car. The 75 bhp 1275 cc engine made the S a 100 mph (160 kmh) car. A Mini Cooper was reintroduced in 1990, twenty-three years after the original was dropped!

Lancia Fulvia Coupé

The pretty little coupé was an offshoot from a saloon range, with V4 1.3- or 1.6-litre engines driving the front wheels. Up to 130 bhp was available, and 115 mph (185 kmh) was possible. These were regarded as the last 'real' Lancias before Fiat influences dominated. The Fulvia was also one of the last non-specialized cars to win top-level rallies.

Porsche 911

This type number has covered a wide range of models since 911 production began in 1964, with a flat six air-cooled engine. The 911S (1966–69 model shown) had a 170 bhp engine and was capable of 135 mph (220 kmh). Constantly refined, the 911 was continued into the 1990s, when some of the handling quirks of the earlier cars had been eliminated.

Ford Mk III

This was a civilized road version of the GT40, a dual-purpose road and track car best known for its two Le Mans 24-hour Race victories. The Mk III had full interior trim and a 4.7-litre V8 'detuned' to give a mere 306 bhp! Although it set the pattern for later supercars, it was ahead of the market and few were sold – replicas in the 1980s and '90s were far more successful!

Honda S600

The Japanese company built on its motorcycle experience when it started building cars and its first little sports car was the S500. The S600 was more widely seen, from 1964. Its refined 606 cc engine developed 57 bhp, which was good for 90 mph (145 kmh). It was succeeded by the S800 in 1967.

Datsun 240Z

Another model that showed the world Japan could build real sports cars, the 240Z was listed 1969–73. It was well equipped, with independent suspension all round, and styled by a European specialist. Most export versions had 2.4-litre engines, and could reach 125 mph (200 kmh). The 240Z gained a rally reputation although victories were few.

MG MGB GTV8

More than 125,000 MGB GTs were built, but only 591 with the Rover 3.5-litre V8 to give a 125 mph (200 kmh) top speed. This well-balanced sports car became sought-after; then, in 1992, Rover 're-invented' a sports MG with the V8.

Morgan Plus 8

Morgans may recall the 1930s in some respects, but the engineering is up to date. With little modification, an existing chassis was suitable for the Rover 3.5-litre V8. Its power rating was increased from 143 bhp in the first Plus 8 in 1968 to 190 bhp in this Vitesse, to give performance closely matching the MGB GTV8.

Ford Capri

In Europe, Ford adopted the Mustang 'long-bonnet' lines for its 1969 Capri which was to appear with many options and, in some forms, was a distinctly sporting coupé. This 1600 GT was a 100 mph (160 kmh) car. The Capri II with a roomier and smoother body took over in 1974.

Renault 6

The 6 filled a market gap for Renault, using some components from the 4 (page 35), with 845 cc or 1108 cc engines driving the front wheels, in a more refined utilitarian car. It was produced for twelve years, with more than 1¾ million sold.

Volvo 164

The square-nose Volvo shape that was to become familiar was introduced with the 144 in 1966 and, two years later, a six cylinder 3-litre engine was squeezed in to produce the 164. Fuel injection was added in 1972 to increase output to 160 bhp, making this comfortable, if unexciting, saloon a 120 mph (190 kmh) car.

Audi 80

The Audi name was revived in the 1960s and this was to become the luxury marque of the VW group in 1965. Its first models in this new existence were competent saloons designated according to engine – 60 (1.? litres), 70 and 80 (1.7 litres), and 90 (1.? litres). The 80 shown was a 95 mph (15? kmh) car.

Peugeot 204

Peugeot's first front-wheel drive car came in 1965, although it did not reach some markets until much later. The 1.1-litre engines (or a 1.4-litre diesel) were mounted transversely, in the Mini fashion. With the petrol unit, 85 mph (135 kmh) was possible. Most were saloons or estate cars; this attractive cabriolet is rare.

Opel Kadett

General Motors' German equivalent to the Vauxhall Viva, the Kadett was a wholly orthodox front engine/rear-wheel drive small saloon, coupé, or estate car launched in 1965. Engine options were 993 cc, 1.1, or 1.2 litres, the larger giving an 80 mph (130 kmh) top speed. This first Kadett style lasted until 1973, and by then more than 2½ million had been sold.

Peugeot 304

Engine size and fittings put this Peugeot in a class above the 204, or the Kadett, while the styling echoed the larger Peugeot 504. This was another worthwhile car, although hardly exciting (especially the sluggish diesel version). It outlasted the 204, being listed 1969–80; the 304S from 1973 was a 90 mph (145 kmh) car.

Fiat Panda

Square-cut lines characterize the Panda hatchback, but helped make the most of interior space in this small Fiat for the 1980s, and beyond. For the Italian market, there was a 652 cc version, but most early export cars had a 903 cc unit, before new FIRE 769/999 cc power units came. The early suspension, which gave an uncomfortable ride, was replaced too. Beyond that, there was a four-wheel drive version, although this was not powerful enough to be an all-round off-road car.

Fiat Uno

Launched in 1983, with neatly styled hatchback body the Uno became Europe' best-selling car in its class Listed with a range of engine from 903 cc to 1.3 litres, wit a diesel option and, from 198 the Turbo – in 1990, a 1.4 litre 118 bhp Turbo wa offered, with a 123 mph (19 kmh) capability. For six year from 1987 the Selecta versio had a continuously variabl automatic transmission.

Volkswagen Golf

The first Golf came in 1974, taking the place of the Beetle in VW's European operations. Neat hatchback styling was by Giugiaro; the transverse water-cooled engines drove the front wheels. GTi was the first 'hot hatch' (1975–83), and the diesel Golf was one of the most acceptable of the type. It sold by the million before being replaced by Golf 2 in 1983.

Volkswagen Polo

The smallest of VW's 'superminis', in many respects this was a scaled-down Golf that was listed in three-door form, 1975–81. There were three engines, 895 cc, 1.1 litres, and 1.3 litres. The 1.1 was an 85 mph (135 kmh) car, with good handling and fairly basic interior. It sold well, before a new-generation Polo took its place for the rest of the 1980s.

Ford Fiesta

Ford's first front-wheel drive car, its first 'supermini', came in 1976 and was built in Britain, Germany, and Spain. The three-door, four-seat hatchback layout was standard, but there were many detail variations as the usual keen Ford marketing policies were followed. Most had 957 cc or 1.1-litre engines, but Fiestas with 1.3- and 1.5-litre units were also listed. A facelift came in 1983.

Mercedes-Benz 600

Far removed from minis, the enormous 600 was intended for heads of state and industrialist – hence, between 1964 and 1981 just 2677 were sold. The standard version was 5.54 metre (18 ft) long, and there was a 6.42-metre (20-ft) limousine. A 6.3-litre V8 propelled it, then was air suspension, and power assistance for seat adjustment, window adjustment, and other functions.

Lincoln Continental

Through the 1970s, Continentals were very large – 'down-sizing' did not come until 1980. Mk III to Mk V (illustrated) were built in two-door coupé form, with four seats – in a car that was 5.92-metres (19.5 ft) long! Engines were V8s, of 6.6 litres or 7.5 litres, neither very powerful because of US emissions and fuel consumption restrictions (the 6.6-litre unit gave 166 bhp at the end of the Mk V's life).

Jaguar XJ12 *(above)*

In many respects, this was an exemplary car, let down by the thirst of its 5.3-litre V12 engine. That was installed in the shell of the existing XJ6, and soon there was a long-wheelbase variant (as well as the badge-engineered Daimler Double Six). The V12 was rated at 253 bhp, was smooth and silent, gave a 150 mph (240 kmh) top speed. The Series I car came in 1972, and gave way to the upgraded Series II model in 1973.

Opel Senator

The big models in the General Motors' European range for ten years from 1978 were the Opel Senator saloon and Monza fastback (illustrated), with the Vauxhall versions both named Royale (1978–82). These conventional and comfortable cars had 2.5- or 3-litre straight six engines, the larger giving a speed approaching 130 mph (205 kmh).

Mercedes-Benz 280SL

A new class of roadster was introduced by Mercedes in 1963, and lasted through to the next decade. All had straight six engines, the first (230SL) in 2.3-litre form with the 2.5-litre 250SL coming in 1966, and the 280SL (illustrated) with a 2.8-litre 170bhp power plant following in 1978. This largest version had a 114 mph (183 kmh) top speed. These were touring cars, with few sports characteristics.

NSU Ro80

The Ro80 still looks handsome, but its twin-rotor Wankel engine gave endless trouble, undermining a car that was refined in other respects. NSU persevered 1968–77, but their failure to solve the engine-sealing problem meant that the brief line ended (meanwhile NSU had amalgamated with Audi in 1969). It was left to Mazda in Japan to make a lasting success of the rotary engine. Some surviving Ro80s have conventional piston engines under their sleek bonnets.

Ferrari 365 GTB/4

Unofficially 'Daytona', this was the last of the great front-engined Ferraris – later types were not so highly rated. Just over 1400 were built, 1968–74, 127 of them soft-tops which were coveted and led to unofficial coupé conversions. The GTB/4 had superb Pininfarina body lines, and it was powered by a 4.4-litre V12, which gave 170 plus mph (275 kmh).

Ferrari Dino 246GT

The 'little Ferrari' was strictly a two-seater, with its 2.4-litre V6 behind the cockpit.
followed on from the first of this new Ferrari generation, a 2-litre model that was badge
'Dino'. With 2.4 litres it was a 150 mph (240 kmh) car, nimbler than most Ferraris. The firs
of the 4000 built came in 1969, and it gave way to the sleeker 308 GT4 in 1977.

Aston Martin V8

At the other end of th
sporting size and weigh
scale from the little Ferrar
this car was launched in 196
as the DBS V8, but wa
renamed after David Brow
sold out. This attractiv
Volante (Aston's name fc
its soft-tops) came in 1973
A 5.3-litre V8 propelled th
standard cars to 145 mpl
(233 kmh) and there wa
more potent 'Vantage
version.

Citroën SM

This attempt to add a high-performance model to the Citroën range was one outcome of the short-lived liaison with Maserati, whose main contribution was the V6 engine, a quad-cam 2.7-/3.0-litre unit. An oddity was headlamps which turned with the steering. Production reached 12,920 (1970–75) before company changes led to its demise.

Pontiac TransAm

Closely related to the Chevrolet Camaro, this Firebird variant owed its name to a US race series; all were coupés and, with changing specifications, were run through the 1970s and '80s. The most potent, in the mid-1970s, had V8s as large as 7.4 litres, but the engine in the 1987 car shown was a 5.7-litre, 213 bhp unit. It was capable of 130 mph (210 kmh).

Porsche 928

The German company's front-engined supercar came in 1977, with a new 4.5-litre V8, and the option of a Mercedes automatic transmission – but then it was not listed as a sports car. The 928S soon came, with a 4.7-litre engine; then, in 1986, there was a 5-litre version. That was a 170 mph (274 kmh) car, whereas the original 928 had a 143 mph (230 kmh) top speed.

Alfa Romeo GTV

This long-lived Alfa coupé body was designed by Giugiaro for the Giulia Sprint in the early 1960s, was continued for the GTV models from 1966 on into the 1970s, the line ending with the 2000 GTV, 1971–77. There were several variations, but these cars all had a sporting appeal, while the GTA and GTAm versions were successful circuit cars.

Alfa Romeo 33

The 33 launched in saloon form in 1983 and in this 33 Sportwagon guise two years later. This normally had front wheel drive in common with the saloons, and 1.5- or 1.7-litre engines, while there was a four-wheel drive version. Performance was good – the 1.7-litre Sportwagon could reach 120 mph (190 kmh).

Alpine A110

Jean Redélé started the Renault line in 1955, and this French sporting marque lasted into the 1990s, from 1974 as a Renault subsidiary. The A110 of 1963 established the Alpine coupé lines, with a backbone chassis and fibreglass bodywork. The Renault 1.1-litre engine was at the rear; by the time production ended in 1977 engines up to 1.8 litres were used.

Matra Djet

When aerospace company Matra took over René Bonnet's concern in 1964, it continued with his Djet cars, as the Matra-Bonnet Djet 6. This was another little rear-engined coupé, with a backbone chassis and fibreglass body. Late versions had 1.3-litre engines rated at 103 bhp, so they were lively cars.

Matra Bagheera

This was unusual in its three-abreast seating, with the driver on the left and two narrower seats to his right. It was introduced in 1973 with a 1.3-litre 84 bhp Simca engine, while the 'S' that came in 1977 had a 1.4-litre 90 bhp unit that gave over 110 mph (180 kmh). The Bagheera was marketed as a Matra-Simca until 1979, and as a Talbot-Matra for its last year.

Porsche Turbo

Basically this was another 911 variant, announced in 1975 and known as the Turbo in its 197_
form. Porsche's flat six engine was enlarged to 3.3 litres, to give 300 bhp and a top speed of 16_
mph (260 kmh); by 1990, power was up to 320 bhp, and the Turbo could attain 168 mph (27_
kmh). Outwardly, the car was distinguished by its large 'tea-tray' rear aerofoil.

Audi Quattro

The four-wheel drive
Quattro made a sensationa_
debut in 1980, and led to a
range of models (hence
'quattro' came to be use_
for the family). It transformed international rallies_
Although it was a large and
heavy car, a turbocharge_
2.1-litre engine propelled i_
to 132 mph (212 kmh)_
Production ended in 1991.

Porsche 911 Cabriolet

'Soft-top' sports cars have featured in Porsche's wide and long-lasting 911 range, from the first to the Turbos, and including this potent 911SC. This variant was introduced in 1978, with a 2.7-litre flat six engine but, by the time the cabriolet came in 1982, capacity was up to 3 litres, and the car could reach 140 mph (225 kmh).

Porsche 944

This 1982 car looked like Porsche's first front-engined model, 924. But it had a new twin-cam four-cylinder engine, initially in 2.5-/2.7-litre form, but a 3-litre unit in the S2 by the end of the decade. The fastest 944 was the 157 mph (250 kmh) Turbo, 1985–91. The Turbo was offered in 2+2 coupé form, the other 944s as coupés or cabriolets.

Triumph TR7

This all-new model in the TR series came in 1975 in two-seat coupé form – the more desirable convertible illustrated did not appear until 1979, and TR7 production ended in 1981. Purists did not like the car's lines, yet it sold better than any other TR. The 2-litre four-cylinder engine gave a 110 mph (176 kmh) top speed.

Mercedes-Benz 500SEC

Mercedes' top-of-the-range coupé for the early 1980 was a quiet and very well equipped grand touring car. The lines were clean and balanced, road manners and performance excellent. It was introduced in 1981, with a 5-litre V8 giving it a top speed of 142 mph (228 kmh).

Mazda RX7

Mazda continued to develop the Wankel rotary engine after other companies had abandoned it and, in 1978, completed its millionth rotary car, an RX7. A second-generation RX7, with more rounded lines, came in 1986, and this turbo version made its debut in 1991. It is a 156 mph (250 kmh) car.

Lotus Esprit

The first Esprit made its debut in 1976, this first turbocharged version in 1980. The basic 2174 cc four-cylinder engine was revised, and a Garrett turbo boosted output to 210 bhp making this a 148 mph (238 kmh) car, while a 1986 improvement to 215 bhp lifted maximum speed above 150 mph (240 kmh).

Renault 5 Turbo

Save in details like the wide wheels and air intakes behind the doors, this looked like a Renault 5. But it was a two-seater, with the engine behind the driver, the suspension was new, some had aluminium bodies, and so on: It was a 'special' created to meet competition regulations, and its 1.3-litre turbo engine made it a 125 mph (200 kmh) car.

Alpine A610

The Alpine line of rear-engined GT coupés ended with this model, a refinement of the backbone chassis theme associated with the marque since 1959. A610 was introduced with a PRV 2.7-litre V6 in 1985; the 3-litre turbocharged version took its place in 1991, and made this a 165 mph (265 kmh) car.

Lamborghini Countach

This head-turning two-seat supercar first appeared in 1974. In the 1980s, its Bertone-styled lines were not improved by aerodynamic additions and large engine air intakes. With the first 4-litre V12, the LP400 was a 170 mph (270 kmh) car; with a 5-litre engine in the LP500 top speed was around 180 mph (285 kmh). The Countach lasted into the 1990s.

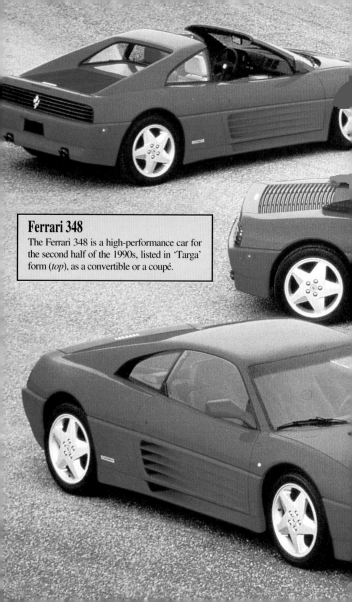

Ferrari 348
The Ferrari 348 is a high-performance car for the second half of the 1990s, listed in 'Targa' form (*top*), as a convertible or a coupé.

The Modern Generation

AC Cobra

The original Cobra prototype in 1961 comprised an AC Ace chassis and a lightweight 4-litre Ford V8. This 'traditional sports car entered production in 1962, when it could reach 165 mph (265 kmh). The Cobra 289 and 427 of 1965 had 4.7 and 7-litre V8s. AC ended production with a few 428s and, in the next twenty years, more than forty companies offered kit replicas so, in 1994, AC got out the jigs and tooling and started building Cobras again.

Alfa Romeo 164

This sleek Pininfarina-styled saloon topped the Alfa Romeo ranges from its introduction in 1988, heralding the marque's regeneration in the 1990s. The engines (a 2-litre four-cylinder and a 3-litre V6) were mounted transversely and drove the front wheels. The V6 gave this quite large saloon a 138 mph (220 kmh) top speed.

Alfa Romeo 75

This distinctive saloon came two years before the 164, and lasted until 1992. Handling and absolute performance (134 mph/215 kmh top speed with the largest of three engines, a 3-litre V6) were good, but interior layout was against it, so were features like the imprecise rear-mounted gearbox.

Alfa Romeo 155

From its launch in 1992 to 1995, reactions to this Alfa were lukewarm. It had some parts in common with the Fiat Tempra and the Lancia Dedra, with a choice of 1.8-, 2-, and 2.5-litre engines. Many shortcomings were ironed out in the 'New 155' in 1995; in particular, the chassis was better matched to the available engines, a 1.8-litre Twin Spark, the new Alfa 2-litre 16V Twin Spark, and a 2.5-litre V6, which gave a top speed of 134 mph (215 kmh).

Alfa Romeo SZ (*above*)

In 1990 this model was taken as an indication that Alfa Romeo was returning to its roots as a manufacturer of high-performance cars. But its looks were against it. The Zagato-style coupé body was efficient in aerodynamic respects but, from some angles the proportions with deep flanks and shallow glass areas, were very odd. Most of the mechanical parts came from other Alfas, and the 3-litre V6 in a 206 bhp version gave a top speed of 152 mph (243 kmh).

Alfa Romeo Spider (*opposite top*)

There were echoes of the SZ in the styling of the Spider and GTV coupé announced in 1994 and in showrooms in 1995, and the Spider picked up the name used for open sports Alfas 1955–93. The Spider and GTV were greeted as drivers' cars. The soft-top Spider is a true sports car, but better aerodynamics mean that the coupé is slightly faster – with the 2-litre 16V Twin Spark engine, its top speed is 134 mph (215 kmh).

Alfa Romeo 145 (*opposite bottom*)

The 145 and the more conventional five-door 146 are important models in the revival of Alfa fortunes. The 145 is a three-door sports hatchback taking the place of the 33, and it lines follow a wedge theme, with an odd V-shape lower edge to the rear window; the interior is also unorthodox, but with comprehensive equipment. Engines are 1.6-litre units, or a 1.7-litre 16V, which gives a 124 mph (198 kmh) top speed.

Aston Martin DB7

One of the most realistic supercars of the 1990s, the DB7 is evidence of the marque's resurgence under Ford ownership. That, and the use of some parts common to other makes, has led to criticism but, in fact, this car is faithful to the DB line. It follows a well-tried layout, with a front-mounted 3.2-litre supercharged six-cylinder engine, rated at 335 bhp and giving a top speed of 165 mph (265 kmh) – not fast enough to make headlines perhaps but, even where it is legal, quite enough for most roads! The 2+2 coupé body has compact, clean lines, and the interior is luxurious.

Aston Martin Virage

This Aston had solid good looks and, under the skin, followed the large-car theme of the 1970s-80s (it made its debut in 1989). The 5.3-litre V8 was uprated to give 310 bhp when introduced and, with the coupé body, that meant a 155 mph (248 kmh) top speed. This car has 2+2 open bodywork.

Audi 80

This 80, introduced in 1992, has the same designation as the model on page 48, and is aimed at the same market sector, but it shows the changes needed to maintain a position over more than two decades. It is listed with engines from 1.4 litres to a 2.6-litre V6. Top of the range is a V6 quattro.

Audi 100

Before Audi abandoned its long-lived '100' designations for the A6 range, this slippery new body shape was introduced for 1992. Among the engines listed was a diesel, while the 2.2-litre Tdi in the coming S6 was offered with a six-speed gearbox.

Audi 100 quattro

Inevitably, cars in the 100 series were available in 'quattro' (four-wheel drive) form, including this estate car. This was aimed at the executive market. It shared the five- or six-cylinder power units with most of the range.

Audi coupé quattro

This sleek two-door, four-seat coupé took on the role of the classic 1983–89 Quattro, and was based on the 80/90 models with a choice of four- or five-cylinder engines (with the latter in 2.3-litre form it was a 137 mph/220 kmh car). It had much better handling qualities than the old model.

Convertibles were very much in favour in the 1990s, from mass-production popular models to the most exclusive, ultra-expensive types. The **Audi A6 Cabriolet** (*opposite*) originally had a 2.3-litre engine, but was uprated with a 2.6-litre unit in 1994. The **Bentley Azure** was a sensational newcomer in 1995. It used mechanical components from the range, including the 6750 cc 385 bhp V8 (top speed around 150 mph/240 kmh), with a neat automatic soft-top, a sumptuous interior and splendid body lines.

Bentley Continental R

When it was introduced in 1991, this was the first Bentley with an all-new and exclusive body since 1952 (it has mechanical components in common with Rolls-Royce models). It is a two-door coupé with sumptuous accommodation and four full seats, without the compromises found in the rear seats of many coupés. A 6.75-litre turbocharged engine gives a top speed of 145 mph (230 kmh).

Bentley Continental S1

This earlier Continental was a top-of-the-range car in the late 1950s. It was supplied to coachbuilders in chassis form, and most of the 43 built had two-door saloon bodies by Mulliner or Park Ward, or rare drophead coupés by Park Ward. The engine was a 4.9-litre straight six.

BMW Z1

This odd little sporting fun car was so well received as a 'show car' that BMW put it into production, but stood by its intention to build only 8000 1986–91). A two-seater with little luggage space or weather protection, and doors that slid down to open, it had a 2.5-litre engine and could reach 140 mph (225 kmh). In 1995 BMW announced the more realistic 1.8-litre Z3 Roadster.

BMW M3

The high-performance variant in the 3-series range, the M3 had a four-cylinder engine rated at 215 bhp in the second year of production (1989 – it ran until 1991). It was a 143 mph (230 kmh) car in standard form, with many competition-inspired transmission and suspension components.

BMW 7-series

The 7-series cars, 1986–94, were offered with a variety of engines – 3- and 3.4-litre straight sixes, a 5-litre V12 from 1987, and, in the early 1990s, V8s of 3 and 4 litres that had high ratings in the executive class. The larger V8 gave a 145 mph (232 kmh) top speed. Equipment lists for these luxurious cars seemed endless.

BMW 5-series

A 'new-look' 5-series came in 1988, with elegant overall lines at a small cost in cabin and boot space, and initially with a range of six-cylinder engines, then a V8 in the 1990s. In 1994 there were eight basic numbered versions, and several times that number of variants when permutations of saloon and estate ('Touring') bodies and engines were taken into account.

BMW 850

The 8-series cars (840 and 850) were the BMW flagship models in the early 1990s, with 5- or 5.6-litre V12s, an electronically limited top speed of 155 mph (250 kmh), six-speed manual or four-speed automatic gearboxes, evidence of very high technology throughout and luxurious interiors. Yet most critics preferred the 7-series cars.

Bristol

The Beaufighter convertible (*left*) and the two-door coupé Britannia/Brigand (*right*) owed their names to famous Bristol aircraft. All three types had 5.9-litre Chrysler V8s, in turbocharged form in late Beaufighters and in the Brigand. Bristols are made in very small numbers, but over long periods (the Beaufighter 1980–92); the

Blenheim, which succeeded this trio, followed very similar lines.

Caterham Super Seven

In 1973 Caterham acquired the rights to build the exciting but simple sports car launched as the Lotus Seven in 1957, and has continued the line ever since. The cars still look like the Lotus original, but the design has been completely re-engineered, and powered by engines from Ford, Rover, and since 1991, Vauxhall, in varying states of tune. All have given this light car exciting performance, which is coupled with outstanding road-holding.

Bugatti EB110

As the 1990s opened, an Italian industrialist chose to revive the name of the once-famous but modestly successful Bugatti marque for a new supercar. This EB110 made its debut in 1991, proving to be a complex, four-wheel drive, two-seater coupé, with a 3.5-litre V12 that had four turbochargers. It was heavy – and looked it – and the cockpit was cramped. A top speed of 212 mph (342 kmh) was claimed. A more sporting version was not prominent in racing, and EB110 sales were disappointing in the limited supercar market.

Chrysler Viper

Here was a car that appeared in 1989 but would have fitted into the motoring scene three decades earlier – an unashamedly muscular two-seater with distinctive styling. Its 406 bhp V10 engine had truck origins and was mounted ahead of the cockpit; it gave a claimed 165 mph (265 kmh) top speed, with dragster acceleration. The Viper carries a Dodge badge in the United States but is a Chrysler in Europe. A hardtop was developed for it in England.

Citroën XM

The XM hatchback was launched in 1989 and this estate car followed in 1991. These a
complex cars, for example with computer-controlled self-levelling oleo-pneumat
suspension. Engines include a 2-litre four-cylinder unit, 2.1- and 2.5-litre diesels, and a 2
litre V6. The larger diesel gives 124 mph (198 kmh), the V6 gives 136 mph (218 kmh), an
these cars have great carrying capacity.

Citroën ZX

Citroën's 1990s entry into
popular, and fiercely con
tested, market class gaine
a reputation for outstandin
handling and adequa
performance, to set again
drawbacks, such as in rea
space. There were four bas
engines, the 1.9-litre dies
having a turbocharger optic
(in that form, the ZX is goc
for 115 mph/185 kmh).

Citroën BX

Like the other recent Citroëns with an 'X' in the designation, the BX was listed in hatchback or estate car forms (from 1982 and 1985 respectively), and both types were to become available with four-wheel drive. There was a range of engines, the smallest (1.4 litres) available only in the saloon, while, at the other extreme, there was a 16-valve 1.9-litre unit giving the GTi a 134 mph (214 kmh) top speed.

Citroën Xantia

The Xantia took over as the BX came to the end of its life in 1993, and in most forms was welcomed as a refined and lively car. Once again, the diesel version was praised. The sophisticated Hydractive II suspension was specified for the top models, and gave excellent ride qualities on all surfaces.

Daewoo Nexia

This Korean manufacturer announced its entry into Britain late in 1994, when its novel marketing policy attracted more attention than its two straightforward models. The smallest of these, the Nexia, is a 1.5-litre family car, in saloon or three/four-door hatchback form resembling earlier Vauxhall Astras. The Nexia is capable of just over 100 mph (160 kmh)

Daihatsu Hijet

Most MPVs are large vehicles but, in 1995 Daihatsu introduced this compact six-seater reminiscent of the Fiat Multipla of the 1950s (then described as a forward control minibus because the term 'people carrier', or MPV, had not been thought of). There is a link, as the van-based Hijet is built in Italy. It has a 993 cc three-cylinder engine.

Daihatsu Applause

The Applause combined the appearance of a saloon with the convenience of a five-door hatchback. In other respects, it was regarded as a well-equipped but undistinguished medium car. The all-alloy fuel-injection 1.6-litre engine gave a top speed of 110 mph (175 kmh).

Daihatsu Charade

This hatchback was first imported to Europe in 1981, with 50 bhp petrol or 37 bhp diesel three-cylinder engines of 993 cc, which gave outstanding economy. These were retained in the 1987–93 version illustrated, and a 1.3-litre four-cylinder engine was added to the range, to give a 103 mph (165 kmh) top speed. The 993 cc GTi version could reach 113 mph (180 kmh). A Charade saloon came for 1994.

Daihatsu Fourtrak

Designed to fill a gap between small off-road vehicles and large types, the Fourtrak came in 1985. It was listed in three-door form, with two petrol and two diesel engine options. In 1994 the Fourtrak independent 2.8TDS was introduced, to give a diesel-powered equivalent to the leisure-oriented Sporttrak.

Ferrari Mondial *(above)*

The Mondial 8 of 1980–89 was Ferrari's first 'world car', intended to meet regulations in most countries. A convertible was built 1984–94. Meanwhile, the Mondial shown was introduced in 1989, with outwardly similar lines concealing many mechanical changes, such as the 3.4-litre V8 mounted fore-and-aft rather than transversely. This was a 158 mph (253 kmh) car.

Ferrari F40 *(below and opposite top)*

The designation marked 40 years of Ferrari cars, and, during its life (1988–92), the supercar was the world's fastest road car. Its twin-turbo 3-litre V8 was rated at 478 bhp in normal form, and much more power was available with race preparation (although it was not a notably successful circuit car). Top speed of the normal F40 was 201 mph (322 kmh).

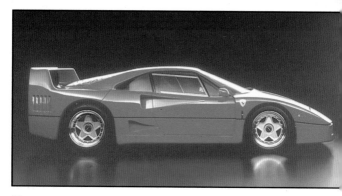

Ferrari F40 (continued)

The chassis and engine of the F40 were based on the 288GTO and, as so often with Ferraris, the lines of the body were by Pininfarina, this time with more aerodynamicist input. The body panels were in carbon composites, for strength and lightness – and incidentally leading to a noisy cabin. This had just two seats, and was spartan. Together, the side shot on page 88 and this view give an impression of the F40's aerodynamic lines.

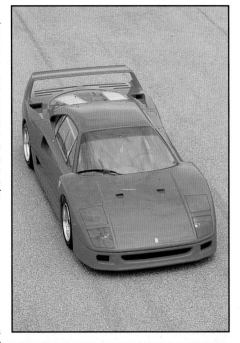

Ferrari 512TR

In a Ferrari tradition, this supercar had a 12-cylinder engine: '512' for the capacity and number of cylinders, 'TR' an echo of the Testa Rossa ('Red Head') name first used on a Ferrari engine in the 1950s. Mounted behind the cockpit, the 4.9-litre unit was rated at 428 bhp, giving the 512TR a 175 mph (280 kmh) top speed, to complement excellent handling and ride qualities.

Fiat Tipo

The unusual lines made for generous interior space and, from its introduction in 1988, all the exterior body panels of the Tipo were galvanized to guard against corrosion. Until 1993 only five-door bodies were built, then a three-door version was introduced. Three petrol engines and two diesels were listed, with 1.8- and 2-litre 16-valve engines coming in

the 1990s; before that, the 1.9-litre turbo-diesel version was the fastest (106 mph/170 kmh).

Fiat Croma

The top-of-the-range Fiat as the 1980s ended, this front-wheel drive, five-door car was available with three versions of a twin-cam 2-litre engine, rated at 90 bhp (carburettors), 120 bhp (fuel injection), and 155 bhp (turbocharged). The latter gave the Croma a 131 mph (210 kmh) top speed but, like most large Fiats, it was only modestly successful.

Fiat Punto

'Car of the Year 1995', Punto is a supermini in three-or five-door forms, with a Cabrio (convertible) also available. It has base petrol engines from 1.1 to 1.6 litres, and a 1.7-litre turbo-diesel. Unusual options include a six-speed gearbox or CVT automatic transmission. The 1.4-litre Punto GT is a 129 mph (207 kmh) car.

Fiat Brava

To succeed the Tipo, Fiat announced the mid-class, three-door Bravo and slightly larger five-door Brava in 1995. The names were chosen because they are understood in all languages. Outwardly, the lines are rounded in a general 1990s style, while the interiors are a little more roomy than in the Tipo. In a range of twenty-four variants there are four petrol engine options and two diesel units, from 1.4 to 2 litres.

Fiat Cinquecento

In the Fiat small-car tradition stretching back to the legendary 500 *topolino* of the mid-1930s, the Cinquecento is a surprisingly roomy and agile town car, capable of 87 mph (140 kmh) in its normal 899 cc engine. With a 66 bhp 1.1-litre engine (and some trim changes), it is transformed, with the Cinquecento Sporting, into a great little fun car, around 10 mph (16 kmh) faster than the standard model.

Fiat Coupé

This shapely new Fiat is a 2+2 model with lines that are unusual overall, and in details such as the headlight covers. Its 2-litre engine, which drives through the front wheels, is listed in 142 bhp or 195 bhp turbocharged forms, the latter giving it a maximum speed of 140 mph (225 kmh).

Fiat Barchetta

Another Fiat tradition was perpetuated in 1995 in the Barchetta front-wheel drive sports car which joined a mid-1990s wave from manufacturers such as MG and BMW. The Barchetta floor pan derived from the Punto and the twin-cam 1.7-litre engine, also used in Lancia and Alfa Romeo types, was in 130 bhp tune. This gave Barchetta a 125 mph (200 kmh) capability.

Ford Granada

The Granada topped Ford ranges from 1972. They gave way to this styling in the Granada and Scorpio; then there was another change in the 'New Scorpio' in 1994. The body shown was also used for the 1985–94 4-wd car, which had only 2.8- or 2.9-litre V6 engines – other Granadas, into the early 1990s, could be fitted with smaller four-cylinder units, a 2.4-litre V6, or a 2.5-litre diesel.

Ford Mustang

The original Mustang of 1964 was a 'personal car' with no real sporting pretensions; later in the decade some versions were developed with real high performance, and some racing potential. The fastback variants were most potent, and this Mach 1 of the early 1970s had a 7-litre V8. In 1973, 'down-sizing' made for less exciting smaller Mustangs.

Ford Escort

The first Escort came in 1968 and, in Mk I and Mk II forms, these small/medium Fords were to be built in versions from mundane to championship race and rally cars, before the 'Mk' designations were dropped and competition types set aside as a front-wheel drive Escort came in 1980. Then the styling was changed to eliminate a radiator grille, as in this XR3 (*below*), which had a 1.8-litre, 128 bhp engine giving a 125 mph (200 kmh) top speed.

The **RS2000** (*bottom*) had a 2-litre twin-cam engine rated at 150 bhp in 1991, which gave most gain in acceleration, as maximum speed only just topped 130 mph (209 kmh). Other components, such as the suspension, were uprated to make this Escort an enthusiast driver's car – at a price.

Most manufacturers of small/medium cars added soft-tops to their ranges in the second half of the 1980s, often using specialist coachbuilders to undertake conversions (Ford and VW used Karmann). Conversion usually involved some loss of space because of strengthening needed. The first **Escort cabriolet** (*opposite top*) came in 1984.

Ford Sierra

The Sierra effectively took the place of the Cortina, becoming familiar on European roads from the first 'jelly mould' car in 1982. The revised version shown, with new bonnet line and wrap-round headlight/indicator units, came in 1987. There were hatchbacks and estate cars, and a four-door saloon that was named Sapphire for the British market. Normally aspirated engines from 1.6 to 2 litres (plus a 2.3-litre diesel) were listed, but the Sapphire RS Cosworth had a twin-cam 220 bhp unit in 1990–92 (top speed 143 mph/230 kmh).

Ford Maverick

This is a compromise vehicle, an attempt to combine road-car qualities with off-road capabilities, with the internal refinement of the former and inevitably the high build of the latter type. It has useful load-carrying and towing qualities, in 'short' (three-door) and 'long' (five-door) forms. Engines are a 2.4-litre petrol unit, giving a top speed of almost 100 mph (160 kmh), or a 2.7-litre turbo-diesel. The Maverick is one of the collaborative cars of the 1990s, for it was developed by Nissan and is built in Spain.

Ford Scorpio

This striking car replaced the Granada/Scorpio range in 1994, in four-door saloon and estate car forms, with engines from 2 litres to 2.9 litres. The multi-valve version of the large unit gives speeds up to 140 mph (225 kmh). The lines may not be to every taste, but the interior are appropriately roomy and comfortable.

Ford Galaxy

The 1995 entry into the MPV market came as a challenge to established models, particularly the Renault Espace, because the Galaxy offered more for less money at any level. It is the product of a Ford-Volkswagen collaboration, with a Ford 2 litre four-cylinder engine or a VW 2.8-litre V6. A VW version of the car is named Sharan. The Galaxy is built in Portugal, equipment levels are high, and driving qualities good.

Ford Mondeo

The Sierra replacement soon gained an excellent reputation to back up its 1994 Car of the Year selection, versions with a new and compact V6 receiving special praise. Within the 4/5 door saloon, hatchback, and estate car range there is a wide choice of variants, with engines from 1.6 to 2.5 litres, giving speeds from just under 100 mph (160 kmh) to almost 140 mph (224 kmh). The millionth Mondeo was completed in 1995.

Ford Probe

American Fords are rarely marketed through Europe but, when the Probe was introduced in 1992, it was welcomed as a 'new Capri'. Experience proved, however, that this good-looking 2+2 coupé did not fit that image, or comfortably into a European market sector, so sales have been modest. The larger of the two engines, a 2.5-litre V6, gives it a top speed of 134 mph (215 kmh).

Honda Prelude

The Prelude name has been used for 2+2 coupés since the 1970s, despite several styling and mechanical changes. Notably, four-wheel steering became available on the top version as the 1990s opened. The Prelude body shown came in 1992, with a chassis and four-cylinder engines (2–2.3 litres) that were praised. Top speeds ranged from 123 mph (198 kmh) to 139 mph (224 kmh).

Honda Accord

The 1985–89 Aerodeck and 1989–92 saloons were the last Accords before British production started. Although this 'Aerodeck sports estate' was refined and reasonably quick with a 2-litre engine (112 mph/180 kmh), it did not have estate car carrying capacity or sports car performance.

Honda Civic

'Civic' was the name of the first serious Honda saloon introduced into Europe in 1972 and through to the 1990s it was used for a variety of vehicles, including this four-door saloon. It was listed with 1.4- or 1.6-litre 16-valve, four-cylinder engines. The 10 millionth Civic was built in 1995.

Honda Concerto

Family resemblances were strong in this model, although it was designed for Europe with Rover collaboration – there are echoes of the contemporary Rovers. Honda's 1.4-, 1.5-, or 1.6-litre engines were listed, the largest available in sohc or twin-cam form, to give speeds up to 122 mph (195 kmh).

Honda Legend

The Legend saloon and coupé of the early 1990s were Honda's largest models, similar to the Rover 25. They had transverse V6 engines (2.7 litres from 1988, later 3.2 litres giving 140 mph/225 kmh), and these drove through the front wheels. Performance was acceptable but the ride was criticized.

Honda NSX

This was welcomed as a supercar in 1990, the first sports Honda since the little cars of the 1960s. There is a mid-mounted, 3-litre, 274 bhp engine, giving 165 mph (265 kmh), with manual or automatic transmission. The NSX-T open version came in 1995.

Hyundai Lantra

This Korean company built its first car, the Pony, in 1976 and its first in-house design was the 1983 Stella. As the next decade opened, the 1.6-litre, 110 mph (177 kmh) Lantra was launched, with a full equipment level and low price its main assets in a very competitive market sector.

Honda Civic Shuttle

The Civic Shuttle run from 1984 was a 1.5-litre, 100 mph (160 kmh) estate car with an unusually upright body. This was carried through to the version illustrated, which came in 1988. It had 1.4- or 1.6-litre engines, with front-wheel drive or four-wheel drive. The 1995 Shuttle – no longer Civic – is a 2.2-litre MPV with a similar outline.

Honda Civic, *fifth series*

The mid-1990s Civics are the best-selling Japanese cars in their market sector, available in three-, four-, and five-door saloon and hatchback forms, while the US-built Coupé is listed in two trim levels (the CRX is no longer listed as a Civic derivative). Entry-level versions have 1.3-litre engines, the 1.5-litre V-TEC units have that outstanding fuel economy record, while a 1.6-litre engine powers the top-performance hatchbacks (134 mph/215 kmh cars). The ESi saloon and hatch illustrated are equipped to high levels.

Hyundai Sonata

The large car in Hyundai's range in the early 1990s, the Sonata actually came in 1989, before the Lantra on page 103. Its front wheels were driven by Mitsubishi engines, the 1.8- and 2-litre units barely giving adequate performance; the 2.4-litre Sonata being a 112 mph (180 kmh) car. The body had a spacious interior.

Hyundai Scoupe

The turbocharged engine is the strong point of this low-price, front-wheel drive, sports coupé, in its MVTi and 1995 Turbo SE forms (there is also a less powerful Injection SE). The odd name was first used on a coupé built around Pony components in 1989, using Mitsubishi-originated engines. The 1995 power unit is a 1.5-litre Hyundai-designed and built engine, which gives 114 bhp in turbocharged form and a 120 mph (192 kmh) top speed. Ride and handling are not highly rated.

Isuzu Trooper

In its first form, 1987–91, the Trooper was a straightforward, working, off-road vehicle; then it evolved with more emphasis on recreational aspects. As the 1990s opened, it was built in short- and long-wheelbase forms, with three or five doors and powerful petrol or diesel engines (in 1992 a 3.2-litre V6 was introduced, to give a 100 mph/160 kmh road speed). Off-road performance has always been convincing.

Jaguar Sovereign

A true high-performance car, the Sovereign is an offshoot of the XJ6 (*opposite*). Mechanically, it has been constantly refined, to complement the leather and wood atmosphere of the interior. Engines have been 3.2- and 4-litre straight sixes, driving through a ZF automatic gearbox. The larger engine gives a 141 mph (227 kmh) maximum speed.

Jaguar XJ6

A new AJ6 engine and a new body came for the replacement for the Series III cars in 1986, and, as part of a continuous programme of improvement, a decade later the XJ6 had a cleanly restyled body and the AJ16 version of the all-alloy, 16-valve, 3.2-litre engine. This gives a top speed of 139 mph (224 kmh). Meanwhile, in the late 1980s, 2.9-, 3.6-, and 4-litre engines had also been specified for the XJ6.

Jaguar XJS

This is another long-lived Jaguar designation, first used for a coupé on the XJ6 floorpan in 1975. That car had a 5.3-litre V12, and was capable of 152 mph (245 kmh); the 1995 XJS has the V12 in 6-litre form or a 4-litre six, giving speeds of 161 mph (259 kmh) and 147 mph (237 kmh). The XJS cabriolet of 1983–87 had been the first open Jaguar since the E-type, and it was followed (1988–91) by a true convertible.

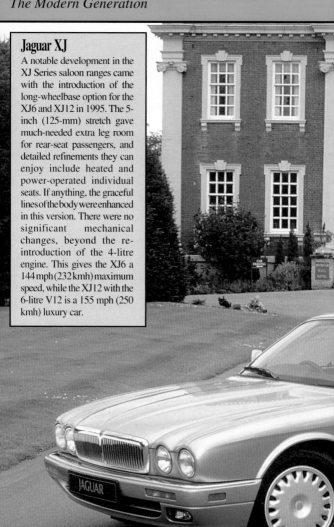

Jaguar XJ

A notable development in the XJ Series saloon ranges came with the introduction of the long-wheelbase option for the XJ6 and XJ12 in 1995. The 5-inch (125-mm) stretch gave much-needed extra leg room for rear-seat passengers, and detailed refinements they can enjoy include heated and power-operated individual seats. If anything, the graceful lines of the body were enhanced in this version. There were no significant mechanical changes, beyond the re-introduction of the 4-litre engine. This gives the XJ6 a 144 mph (232 kmh) maximum speed, while the XJ12 with the 6-litre V12 is a 155 mph (250 kmh) luxury car.

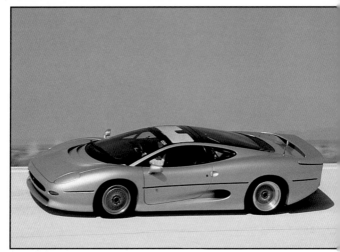

Jaguar XJ220

The forerunner of this supercar was greeted enthusiastically in 1988. It did not evolve as expected, however – worst of all, the production version did not have a V12 but a twin turbocharged V6 that derived from a Rover V8. It was still fast, reaching 212 mph (341 kmh), but lacked one supercar magic ingredient. For a two-seater, it was also large, but that was not reflected in cockpit space. When production did get under way, XJ220 sales failed to come up to expectations.

Jaguar XJS Convertible

Open high-performance cars have always been attractive and few in the 1990s have matched the XJS, first seen as a full convertible in 1988 and here in its 1991 form. This car had a new subframe to eliminate the scuttle shake that spoils some adaptations of closed cars, and there was full electric operation of the folding hood.

Jeep Wrangler

The Wrangler is the modern Jeep that is closest to the image of the classic 1940s military vehicle. But it has 'civilized' elements undreamed of in that original, such as a stout roll cage, power steering, and a hard top (and in the Limited version even leather seats). The low-cost Wrangler has a 2.5-litre engine, the two top versions have 4-litre straight six engines, giving a claimed 100 mph (160 kmh) road speed. In normal road driving the power is transmitted through the two rear wheels, and the 'part time' 4wd system can be engaged while the Jeep is on the move.

Jeep Cherokee

More stylish than the Wrangler, the Cherokee is marketed in three versions – the 2.5 Sport, the 4.0 Limited, and the 4.0 Limited SE. The 4-litre models have automatic transmission, selectable 2wd or 4wd, cruise control, ABS brakes, air conditioning, and so on. Road speed is up to 112 mph (180 kmh).

Kia Pride (*above*)

The Pride was this Korea company's European launc model, in 1991. In fact, it wa the old Mazda 121 that wa dropped in that year, mild reworked and relying on i value-for-money appeal in th supermini category. The 1. litre Pride was a three-do hatchback but the 1.3-litr version could also be bough with five doors. Measure performance was good – 9 mph (148 kmh) top speed – b in aspects such as ride it wa less convincing.

Lada Samara (*above*)

After decades of building obsolescent cars, this was a Russian attempt to compete with European and Japanese small cars. It was a front-wheel drive hatchback, with 1.1-, 1.3-, or 1.5-litre engines, mounted transversely. The middle version could reach 93 mph (150 kmh). The interior was roomy, but the trim and fittings tended to be of poor quality.

ada Niva

he basic Niva was a small
vd vehicle, with utilitarian
uipment. It was revised
r 1995 in this Cossack 4x4
rsion, which has a 1.7-
re fuel-injection engine
d many detailed
echanical improvements.
is a practical off-roader,
ith a useful top-hinged rear
or, but still with interiors
at are far from luxurious.

amborghini LM

his extraordinary vehicle was at the opposite end of the off-road spectrum. It was expected
have military applications as a high-speed, all-terrain machine – some were sold to the
iddle East for that purpose – but turned out to be an exotic off-roader. The production
rsions, launched in 1985 and lasting until 1992, were the LM002 with a front-mounted,
2-litre V12, and the LM004 with a 7.3-litre V12 that had been designed for power boats.
he original intention meant that the LMs had rugged chassis and, in contrast, luxurious air-
onditioned interiors.

Lamborghini Diablo

With this striking supercar, Lamborghini sought to replace the Countach (page 63). It is more curvaceous, but has similar lines, still with the doors opening upwards through mountings at the front. The 5.3-litre V12 had been used in the Countach S, and it was rated at 492 bhp in standard form, or 525 bhp in this 1995 SE. The normal Diablo has rear-wheel drive, but the VT of 1991 boasted 4wd. Claimed top speed of the Diablo is 202 mph (323 kmh).

AC 868 DV

Lancia Delta HF

The first Delta was a five door hatchback in 1980 which appeared in turbo charged form in 1984, and with four-wheel drive in 1987. Rally needs led to the Integrale – and it conquered the rally world – which, in road form, was a car with fine handling and ride as well as performance (with the 210 bhp engine in later cars, it reached 134 mph 215 kmh). In all-round terms, this Lancia matched most sports cars.

Lancia Thema

The first Thema executive saloon was one of the 'Type Four' cars developed by Fiat group companies and Saab (the Fiat Croma, Alfa Romeo 164, and Saab 9000). Originally it had a 2-litre petrol engine or a 2.4-litre diesel; in its short-lived Thema V6 form (1985–88) it had the 2.8-litre PRV V6; the Thema 8-32 of 1988–92 actually had the Ferrari 308 V8. In the 1990s, the Thema has been powered by a 2-litre turbo unit, a 2.85-litre V6, and a 2.5-litre turbo diesel. All these drove through the front wheels. In other respects, this was a conventional car.

Lexus LS400

Toyota created its prestige Lexus marque to compete with European luxury car manufacturers, and, when the LS400 appeared, it was a match for similar models from BMW and Mercedes-Benz. It was announced in 1988, launched in Europe in 1990, and given a facelift in 1993. Build quality is outstanding, it is refined, its 4-litre V8 is remarkably quiet and gives it a 147 mph (235 kmh) maximum speed, and its four-speed automatic transmission is exemplary. There have been detail criticisms of the ride, and its looks are hardly distinguished . . . but it is an outstanding car.

Land Rover Discovery

The Discovery took its place between the Land Rover and the Range Rover in 1989, using the same chassis and power unit. Like every Land Rover since the Jeep-inspired original of 1948, it is a sturdy and practical off-road vehicle, with good road-driving qualities. It had the 3.5-litre all-alloy V8, or a 2.5-litre diesel, with a 3.9-litre version of the V8 coming in 1994. That made it a 105 mph (168 kmh) vehicle, and it had refinements such as a five-speed all-synchromesh gearbox (or four-speed automatic transmission) that few owners would have dreamed of through the first four decades of Land Rover history!

Land Rover Range Rover

This photograph sums up twenty-five years of the Range Rover, with one of the 1970 production vehicles in the foreground, a 1994 Classic in the centre, and the 'New Range Rover' of that year behind it. Throughout, the intention was a well-mannered road and off-road vehicle, and in this it has continually set international standards. The original, however, had 'hose-down' interiors with basic rubber mats, and, since then, Range Rovers have acquired many luxury fittings.

The first Range Rover was listed in three-door form, with a light-alloy 3.5-litre V8, full-time four-wheel drive and a four-speed gearbox. Two more side doors came in 1981, there was an automatic transmission in 1982, and a five-speed manual gearbox in 1983; the Vogue SE, with leather upholstery, air conditioning, and a sun roof appeared in 1988. A 3.9

tre V8 came in 1990, and, in 1994 the 'New Range Rover' had a redesigned 4-litre version or a BMW 2.5-litre turbo diesel). This current model also has air suspension and ABS, and, n 4-litre SE form, reaches 116 mph (185 kmh).

Lotus Elan

Enthusiasts looked to this 1989 front-wheel drive car to restore the Lotus name as a sports car constructor. It had a backbone chassis and composites body, with the option of the double-skinned hard top illustrated, and a 1.6-litre engine in 130 bhp or 165 bhp turbo-charged forms, to give 136 mph (218 kmh). Handling was outstanding.

Lotus Esprit

The first mid-engined Esprit came in 1976, and the Turbo of 1980 brought it into the supercar class, then it was substantially restyled on a stiffer chassis in 1987. These softer lines were carried through to the S4 of 1993, which was distinguished by its five-spoke alloy wheels. A 2.2-litre turbocharged engine mounted behind the cockpit gives the S4S a 160 mph (258 kmh) top speed, while the Sprint 300 reaches 168 mph (270 kmh).

Marcos Mantula

Mantula was Marcos's name for its Rover-engined model introduced in 1984, with this Spyder open two-seater coming two years later. The moulded fibreglass body was mounted on a steel chassis. With a 3.9-litre version of the Rover V8 used from 1989, this was a 150 mph (240 kmh) car. It gave way to the 1992 Mantara Spyder, which was joined by the potent LM500 in 1994.

Mini Marcos

The beefy Marcos sports cars seem well removed from this little coupé, but the spirit behind them is un-changed, and, with some 700 produced 1965–74 (most in kit form), the Mini Marcos was the mainstay of the company in its early years; D&H Fibreglass later built a few, and this little coupé was the inspiration for the Midas.

Maserati 222

Changes of ownership led to changes of policy at this company in the 1980s, bringing in bland coupé, saloon, or convertible lines. This 222 is an example, and the basic body shape by Gandini was continued through to models such as the Shamal and Ghibli of the mid-1990s. These were luxury cars with sports car performance, achieved with variants of four-cylinder and V6 engines.

Mazda 323

The first 323 was Mazda's first front-wheel drive car, in 1981-85. The third body style (illustrated) came in 1989, with three or five doors and a range of engines from 1.3 to 1.8 litres. An all-new 323 was introduced for 1994, and this was available with a compact 2-litre V6.

Mazda 626

A relatively large front-wheel drive car, the 626 came in 1978 and in its third form (from 1987 was to feature a range of bodies. All were very well equipped and the top-of-the-range versions could have four-wheel drive, while the 2-litre GT had four-wheel steering.

Mazda MX-3

This sleek little coupé for the 1990s is listed with a 1.6-litre engine and an automatic gearbox or the much more convincing combination of a 1.8-litre V6 and a five-speed manual gearbox. The chassis and suspension could probably cope with higher speeds than the 124 mph (200 kmh) maximum. The MX-3 is aimed at the 'hot hatch' market.

Mazda MX-5

The wide acceptance of this pretty little sports car is understandable – it is a delight to drive and it recaptures the spirit of open two-seaters of the past, with qualities that are appropriate to the 1990s (it was introduced in 1989). Its first 1.6-litre engine gave it a 114 mph (183 kmh) top speed; the 1.8-litre engine that came in 1994 gave gains in flexibility, but little in speed.

McLaren F1

The F1 set new supercar standards for the 1990s, and even the briefest experience exhausts superlatives. It has a finely styled and aerodynamically efficient body, built with high-tech materials, and a compact and potent 620 bhp, tailor-made BMW V12 drives through a six-speed transaxle. A prototype achieved 231 mph (370 kmh) and the F1's power-to-weight ratio gives it phenomenal acceleration – it can reach 200 mph from rest in 28

seconds. Yet, when larger supercars can just accommodate two people and little luggage, the McLaren is a genuine three-seater, with a passenger on each side of the driver (and slightly behind him or her).

More than that, in its F1 GTR form, not far removed from the road car, it scored McLaren's first victory in the classic Le Mans 24-hour Race, in 1995 (*inset*, the Le Mans-winning car displayed at the Goodwood Festival of Speed, with trophies and road F1s).

Mercedes-Benz SL

This SL500 was introduced in 1989 and, until the SL600 came in 1992, it was the flagship of the SL range. It is still an outstanding car, with a fully automatic soft top (and a hard top) a rollover bar that extends instantly to protect occupants in an accident situation, four- or five-

speed automatic transmission, refinement in every detail, and a centre console with an array of secondary controls. A 5-litre V gives effortless performance, and a 160 mp (257 kmh) top speed.

Mercedes-Benz C class

There are six basic models – 25 variants altogether – in Mercedes' smallest car range, and the C36 AMG with special styling details as well as a 3.6-litre 280 bhp engine (giving 250 kmh/155 mph maximum). The other models run from the 1.8-litre C180 to the 2.8-litre C280, and there are two with diesel engines. Equipment levels are not lavish, but qualities such as the ride on all road surfaces are excellent.

Mercedes-Benz E36 AMG

The mid-range Mercedes (the W124 models) came in 1987 with 2- and 3-litre engines, but this AMG version of the mid-1990s has a 3.6-litre power unit. AMG is a German specialist engineering company that has had links with Mercedes since 1990. Its conversions have larger and more powerful engines than the standard models, and other improvements such as sports suspension and body modifications. This E36 AMG has a top speed governed to 250 kmh/155 mph.

Mercedes-Benz G-wagen

In 1979 this rugged off-roader by Mercedes and Puch, with its plain exterior matching a sparse interior, seemed a German answer to the Range Rover, although it had smaller engines – 2.3 and 2.7 litres and a 3-litre diesel. In its 2.7-litre 280GE form it came closer to the Range Rover. The G illustrated has the slightly softer body lines from 1991, when the 3-litre 300G with a top speed of 102 mph (163 kmh) was introduced.

Mercedes-Benz E class

Mercedes diehards were surprised by the lines of the New E-class in the summer of 1995. The medium-range saloons have a distinctive nose, with four ellipsoid headlights, and rear lines reminiscent of a coupé, as refined aerodynamics were added to weight reduction to improve performance. Engines range from 2- and 2.3-litre fours to a 3-litre straight six. Very high safety levels are claimed (these are the first Mercedes to have side air bags) and there are three equipment versions.

MG MGF

For a dozen years from 1980 it seemed that the last MGB had been the last open MG sports car, then the MG RV8 in 1992 was the first sign of a revival. That was a retrospective car, so the new MGF was widely welcomed in 1995 – marque loyalty is important to success in a limited market sector which saw the debuts of

rival two-seat sports cars from Alfa Romeo, BMW, and Fiat. The MGF is a mid-engined two-seater, using 1.8-litre engines in 1.8i 120 bhp and 1.8i VVC 145 bhp forms. The rest of the specification is thoroughly up to date, although the use of Hydragas suspension came as a surprise. The cockpit is roomy and, unusually for a fairly small mid-engined car, there is adequate luggage space. Claimed top speeds are 120 mph (192 kmh) and 130 mph (208 kmh) for the VVC.

Mini Cooper

This famous model re-appeared in 1990 – production of the normal Mini never stopped of course – and a niche market demand for it continued. In 1990 the 1.3-litre fuel-injection engine was rated at 63 bhp, and in 1995 a John Cooper Garages 'special edition' had an engine producing over 80 bhp, to give a top speed over 100 mph (160 kmh). By that time the interior of the mainstream Mini Cooper had also been improved, so this Cooper version also had external and internal embellishments.

Mini Moke

This little fun derivative of the Mini has an unusual history. It first appeared in military prototype forms, and a production simple utility, or fun, version came in 1964. That lasted for four years, then the Moke was built in Australia, then through to the mid-1980s some were made in Portugal, where Moke Automobili restarted production of the car illustrated in 1991. This version has a 70 mph (112 kmh) capability – quite enough when it is in open form . . .

Mitsubishi Colt

'Colt' was used as a make name when Mitsubishi exports to Europe started in the late 1970s but, a decade later, it was adopted as the model name for small three-door hatchbacks such as the early-1990s pair illustrated. There were 1.3- or 1.5-litre engines, and the GTI with a twin-cam 1.5-litre unit could exceed 120 mph (190 kmh).

Mitsubishi Space Wagon

This practical 'people carrier' in five-door form, with three rows of seats (for seven people), was first seen in 1984. It was well equipped but, with a 1.8-litre petrol or diesel engine, did not have sparkling performance and it could only just reach 100 mph (160 kmh). The mid-1990s 2-litre version is a 112 mph (180 kmh) vehicle.

Mitsubishi Shogun

This very successful four-wheel drive vehicle behaved like a car on the road and had enough power to perform well off-road. Its tough and, with early 3-litre V6 or 2.5-litre turbo diesel, 100 mph (160 kmh) was within reach, and was easily exceeded in second-generation models. To confuse car spotters outside Britain, it is named Pajero in most countries.

Mitsubishi Galant *(above)*

The Galant name dates from the early 1980s, with front-wheel drive types coming in 1984. These tended to be 'executive' cars, with powerful engines and generous equipment standards. In 1989 four-wheel drive and four-wheel steering were added to the advanced specification of the Galant. The 2-litre V6 was refined, smooth, and flexible, and gave a 128 mph (205 kmh) maximum speed.

Mitsubishi Space Runner *(below)*

While it appears to complement the Space Wagon (page 133), the more compact Space Runner is an estate car rather than an MPV with two rows of seats, for five people. With a 1.8-litre petrol engine it is fractionally faster than its 'big brother'. The turbo-diesel version, however, does not quite reach the magic 100 mph (160 kmh).

Nissan Sunny

The first generation Sunny was sold under the Datsun name, 1966–70, the fifth for 1982 were front-wheel drive small cars, and the 1986–91 Sunny came with a variety of bodies and engines This ZX of 1991, with a 1.8-litre engine, could reach 128 mph (205 kmh), and the 2-litre GTi-R of 1992 was very fast.

Nissan Primera

The first British-built Nissan was the 1986–90 Bluebird, and the Primera which followed has gained a reputation for all-round excellence; it appears a little dated, even after a facelift for 1995. Saloon and estate versions have been listed, with 2-litre engines that gave the GSX illustrated a 120 mph (192 mph) top speed, while the T was faster, and all had handling to match those speeds.

Nissan 100NX

Here was a recent Nissan that was not very highly rated by pundits. A 2+2 coupé, it used the Sunny floorpan and suspension as well as its 1.6-litre engine in 95 bhp form. That gave the car a near-competitive top speed (115 mph/185 kmh) in its class, but acceleration was less impressive.

Nissan 200SX

Unlike the 100NX, this mode became a class leader soon afte its 1989 introduction, its twin cam 1.8-litre engine giving it 140 mph (225 kmh) top speed the fastest in class/price terms. was mildly uprated; then a revise version in 1994 was given mo rounded lines and a 2-litre pow unit which raised maximum spee to 146 mph (234 kmh).

Nissan 300ZX

Last of the 'Z' line that was launched in 1969 with the famous Datsun 240Z, this looked a heavier car, and a weighbridge showed that it was. The rounded lines also provided good aerodynamics, and coupled with a 3-litre turbocharged engine meant that it was fast in its 1984–90 form (143 mph/230 kmh); the 1992 type illustrated had a twin-turbo option, and its top speed was restricted to 155 mph (250 kmh).

Nissan Micra

European Car of the Year 1993, the Micra was engineered for Europe at the company's Technical Centre at Cranfield, and is built in Britain. It fills lively supermini and town-car roles, and is listed in three- and five-door forms. Engines of 1 litre or 1.3 litres give 92/106 mph (147/170 kmh) top speeds, but the most impressive technical feature is the optional CVT (Continuous Variable Transmission) computer-controlled system. This is outstandingly smooth (the manual gearchange is highly rated, too). The Micra is well equipped, but its lines already appear dated.

Peugeot 205

A very strong contender in the hatchback class from its 1983 introduction, the 205 has crisp Pininfarina lines, excellent handling and performance, from good in the base versions to exciting in the GTi hot hatch (1984–94 – a 1.6- or 1.9-litre car, capable of 120 mph/192 kmh).

Peugeot 309

Somehow this larger model never gained the appeal of the 205. In part, it owed its origin to a Talbot, acquired when Peugeot took over the British factory. Built in three- and four-door forms, with six petrol engines and a diesel during its 1986–93 life, it was a very sensible car.

Peugeot 405

A handsome medium saloon, European Car of the Year in 1988, available in saloon or estate forms (and a few built with four-wheel drive), this was another very practical car. Most were sold with 1.6- or 1.9-litre engines (top speed 120 mph/192 kmh); there were two diesels. Top of the range was the 1.9-litre twin-cam Mi16, a 132 mph (210 kmh) car.

Peugeot 306

The 306 appeared as a smartly styled three- or five-door hatchback, with engines including the highly rated 1.9-litre turbo diesel; a conventional four-door saloon came in 1995, and the Cabriolet illustrated is the flagship of the range. With a 1.8-litre petrol engine, the hatchback is a 114 mph (182 kmh) car, and with the diesel it reaches 108 mph (173 kmh). Ride and handling are good, as is accommodation, save perhaps in the luggage space of the hatchback.

Peugeot 406

Peugeot's medium saloon for the second half of the 1990s came in autumn 1995, with a long 'three-box' body (engine, passenger compartment, boot) giving lithe lines. In the highest of four trim levels the interior is luxurious, and passive safety equipment is extensive. Initially, there are 1.8- and 2-litre petrol engines and a turbo-diesel version.

Peugeot 106

The 106, and the Renault Cl[io] below, are lively but buzz[y] with surprising space for tw[o] people, adequate for four, an[d] some odd characteristics. Th[e] 1.4-litre diesel-engined 10[6] reaches 85 mph (136 km[h]) while, at the other end of th[e] range, the 1.3-litre 106 Rall[y] is a 118 mph (189 kmh) ca[r] while the 'hot hatch' 1.4-lit[re] XSi is only fractionally slowe[r]

Renault Clio

This challenges the 106 in many markets and, in some forms, is more highly rated. Its 1990 lines are not to every taste. In that launch year there were 1.2- and 1.4-litre engines, with a 1.8 coming in 1991 – in RSi form the 1.8 can reach 120 mph (192 kmh). There is the usual choice of three- or five-door body styles.

Renault Clio Williams

The time-honoured custo[m] of naming a car to explo[it] competition successes [was] followed by Renault in [the] top-of-the-range Clio, to ma[rk] the Grand Prix success [of] Renault-powered William[s] cars. This little hatchback [is] impressive, with a 2-lit[re] engine developing some 15[0] bhp, to give it a top speed ov[er] 130 mph (210+ kmh).

Porsche 911 Carrera 2

The evergreen rear-engined 911 continued through the 1990s, and this Carrera 2 variant came in 1989, in 2+2 coupé, Targa, and cabriolet forms – the fully open version illustrated is a limited-edition car. Its flat-six 3.6-litre engine was in normally aspirated form, and gave a 162 mph (260 kmh) top speed.

orsche 911 Carrera RS

his slightly earlier 911
arrera, with its unattractive
mpact-absorbing bumpers,
as the first to carry an 'RS'
Rennsport) designation since
e early 1970s. Its mechanical
ecification is similar to
arrera 2 but it was a marginally
ower car. Compared with
rlier Carreras, it was a little
ore refined and had a better-
uipped cockpit.

Porsche 968

This supercar has gained a great reputation for handling and for the outright performance from a four-cylinder 3-litre engine (it is capable of more than 150 mph/ 240+ kmh). The Club Sport illustrated is the entry-level 968, with no pretensions to luxury; above it are the Sport, Coupé, and Cabriolet.

Proton Aeroback

Malaysian manufacturer Proton came to Europe in 1988, with a model based on an obsolescent Mitsubishi, and started to build up a value-for-money reputation. The Aeroback followed, in a twelve-model range with Mitsubishi-designed 1.3- and 1.5-litre engines (the larger gave a top speed near 100 mph/160 kmh). The cars were revised in 1992, and these Protons still sold on reliability and value reputations.

Reliant Rialto

Economical three-wheelers were once popular in Britain, for reasons such as a low road tax and a tiny market continued into the 1990s. Apart from ultra-specialists building sportin devices, Reliant was by then the only three-wheel manufacturer, struggling to survive. Rialto and Robin were powered by its own 848 cc engine (in 1963 this had taken the place of the Austin Seven-based unit Reliant had used since 1938). The glass-fibre bodies at lea ensured that these vehicles were rustproof.

Renault 5

here were once sixteen models in the 5 range but, by 1995, only the Campus remained. The 5 might have been overtaken by later designs, but it was a landmark Renault – its success was vital to the company. Built with several engines (up to 1.7 litres in the Supercinque), it had an excellent ride and good interior space.

Renault 19

This model occupied a small/medium place among Renaults, from 1988, in 3/5-door hatchback and later saloon forms, with 1.4- or 1.7-litre petrol engines, or a 1.9-litre diesel. The Azur Cabriolet came in the early 1990s, then 16-valve engine 'Executive' versions (good for 130 mph/208 kmh) before the face-lifted Phase 3 models in 1995.

Renault 25

The 25 topped the Renault lists from 1984 until 1992. Most were upmarket hatchbacks, but there was also a long-wheelbase Limousine version. Four-cylinder engines (2 and 2.2 litres) or V6 units from 2.5 to 2.8 litres drove the front wheels. Top speed with the large engine was 134 mph (215 kmh).

Renault 21

Logic meant that this took its place a level below 25, in 1986. The first saloons were followed by estate cars and a hatchback, with four engine types. The Turbo, with a 175 bhp 2-litre engine, came in 1988 and, two years later, four-wheel drive was adopted for this model (it could reach almost 140 mph/224 kmh.

Renault Espace

Renault's classic MPV wa developed by Matra an launched with a 2-litre engin in 1985; a 2.2-litre and 3-lit V6, and a 2.1-litre turbo diese were to come. The first versio reached 109 mph (174 kmh with the V6, the Espace is a 12 mph (195 kmh) people carrie For a decade after its launc the Espace set the standard f the class.

Renault Safrane

Taking the place of the 25 as the Renault flagship model, in its RXE or V6i V6 3-litre form, the Safrane received mixed reviews. The RXE was a 130 mph (210 kmh) car. In 1995 the range was overhauled, the base introduction model was dropped, and a new Executive 2.5 TD introduced with a 'high-economy' 2.5-litre turbo diesel.

Renault 5 Gordini Turbo

This is a car from Renault's past, carrying the name of a French racing car constructor and tuning wizard, and not to be confused with the fierce little competitions 5 Turbo on page 63. It had a mildly boosted 1.4-litre engine producing 110 bhp, to give a 112 mph (180 kmh) top speed. It came in 1982, very much in the spirit of a reviving company, was renamed Le Car 2 Turbo in 1984, and then gave way to the Supercinque.

Rolls-Royce Silver Spirit

At the other motoring extreme, Rolls-Royce cars continue to offer dignified comfort, and no mean performance for such large vehicles. The Silver Spirit and the Silver Spur (slightly longer, to allow for a division between chauffeur and passengers) were contemporaries of the Renault, introduced in 1980. Production reached 14,366 before an uprated version came in 1989. Both had the R-R all-alloy 6.7-litre V8, giving a quiet maximum speed of 120 mph (192 kmh). There was subtle updating in 1995, and the claimed maximum speed increased to 133 mph (213 kmh).

Rolls-Royce Silver Shadow

The 1965 Silver Shadow was the first-ever Rolls-Royce monocoque production model, and it had self-levelling independent suspension all round. It was launched with the R-R alloy V8 in 6.2-litre form but, in 1970, the 6.75-litre engine took its place. All drove through a GM automatic transmission. More than 19,000 were built (including 2776 long-wheelbase cars) before the Silver Shadow II (*illustrated*) came in 1977. Both types had maximum speeds approaching 120 mph (192 kmh).

Rover Metro

Launched in 1980 as the Austin-Morris Metro, this supermini became a Rover a decade later. Originally it was a three-door 1-/1.3-litre car with components from older models. Capable of 93 mph (149 kmh). As a Rover, it had the K-series 1.1-/1.4-litre engine, and became available with the Continuously Variable Transmission (with the 1.4-litre engine, that was a 100 mph/160 kmh car).

Rover Maestro

Maestro was a practical five-door hatch, introduced with some aged components in 1983. An estate came in 198 and, among new engines, a 2 litre turbo diesel was introduced late in 1988 (that gave a 101 mph/163 kmh top speed while the contemporary 2 litre petrol-engined Maestro reached 109 mph/175 kmh.

Rover 200

The first 200 series cars were front-engined, rear-drive saloons, and the Honda association continued in this front-wheel drive type, announced late in 1989. The hatch styling was complemented by the 220 coupé and a cabriolet from 1992. The 220i turbo coupé had 2 litres and, in 1993, was Britain's cheapest 150 mph (240 kmh) car.

Rover 400

The 400 saloons followed the 200 in 1990, and also used 1.4-/1.6-litre engines, together with a 1.8-litre turbo diesel and a 2-litre unit in the MI6i Sport (a 127 mph/204 kmh car). Generally, these were polished medium cars. The revised 400 Series was introduced with 1.4-/1.6-litre five-door models in 1995, with four-door saloons and more engines for 1996.

Rover 800

Introduced in 1986 as Rover's flagship range, with 2-litre four-cylinder engines or a Honda 6-litre V6. The revised body (illustrated) and a coupé came in 1992, then there was the 00 Vitesse Sport in 1994. Above all, the 800s have been successful executive saloons, with the smallest engine (in the 821i) giving a top speed of 125 mph (200 kmh).

Rover 100

This series took over from the Metro, re-engineered to a degree, still with K-series engine in 1.1- and 1.4-litre capacities, and with three- or five-door bodies. A distinctive feature was the smart new nose, here shown on the 1995 cabriolet variant. As introduced in 1994, the 114 version was capable of 103 mph (165 kmh).

Rover 600

based on the Honda Accord, but with intangible assets, and interior furnishings and fittings that set it apart from the Japanese car, in the turbocharged 620ti version, this was a 140+ mph (225+ kmh) GT car. The base 621i is no slouch, reaching 122 mph (195 kmh). As an alternative to the four petrol-engined models, the version illustrated has the Rover L-series -litre diesel engine.

Saab 900

The designation has been used by the Swedish company since 1978, and variations, suc
as the Turbo and a very attractive convertible, appeared through the 1980s. A new 900 rang
that came in 1993 retained the 'family image' and some Saab individuality, with three- an
five-door coupé hatchbacks and a convertible. As ever with Saabs, these were aerodynamicall

ficient, had comprehensive safety equipment, and well-laid-out cabins – on a Vauxhall Cavalier floorpan! The engines were 2-/2.3-litre units and a refined 2.5-litre V6, which some critics preferred to the smaller, but more powerful, turbocharged engines. The model illustrated is a 1995 900 SE Turbo Coupé.

Saab 9000

These 4/5-door cars followed Saab efficiency and safety traditions and have elements in common with Fiat group models in the 'Type Four' programme. The image might have been staid, but performance with the turbo 2-litre engine at the 1985 introduction could be brisk. A 2.3-litre version was available from 1989, and the 3-litre V6 that came

for 1994 gave a 130 mph (208 kmh) top speed, compared with the 2.3-litre Turbo, which could reach 140 mph (225 kmh).

SEAT Toledo

Volkswagen engineering benefits this capable middle-range Spanish car for the 1990s. In five-door form, is listed with engines from 1.6 to 2 litres, giving speed from 105 mph (168 kmh) 122 mph (195 kmh), with an even quicker GT version. The basic versions have value-for-money appeal.

SEAT Ibiza (*opposite top*)

This 11-model supermini range has body styling by Giugiaro and is engineered by VW. There are six different engines, from the workaday 1-litre unit that gives 85 mph (135 kmh) to a 1.8-litre 16-valve engine rated at 130 bhp and giving a 130 mph (208 kmh) top speed. The diesel-engined version is highly rated.

SEAT Cordoba (*opposite bottom*)

A compact saloon, the Cordoba complements the Toledo hatchbacks, with lines that are distinctive (and the GTi picked out, with its alloy wheels and tail spoiler). Passenger and luggage space good. The 1.6-litre versions with petrol and turbo diesel Cordobas both reach 105 mph (168 kmh), while the GTi is a 123 mph (19 kmh) car – a sports saloon.

SsangYong Musso

The distributors for this Korean-built 4x4 recognize that this type of vehicle spends mo of its time on normal roads, and therefore stress its excellent drag figure, which could see unimportant to an off-roader. SsangYong refer to the Musso as a 'recreational vehicle'. was styled in Britain, and it uses Mercedes-Benz engines (a five-cylinder 2.9-litre diesel the late-1993 launch model, with a petrol straight six following), and Mercedes automa transmission is an option. The Musso is heavily built, so performance with the diesel is n scintillating (90 mph/145 kmh maximum).

Subaru Impreza

Essentially, Impreza is small/medium four-whe drive car, and the two-whe drive version (listed with t least-powerful 1.6-lit engine) was almost an afte thought. There are 4-/5-do bodies, with flat-fo (horizontally oppose engines of 1.6 and 1.8 litr respectively. Top of t range is this 2-litre Turbo 142 mph (228 kmh) car. the Impreza backgrou there is a successful inte national rally record.

Skoda Favorit

The front-wheel drive Favorit was launched in 1989, with this estate car following in 1991 – the year Volkswagen took an interest in this long-established Czech company. Its reputation for character-less cars was laid to rest. Favorits have 1.3-litre all-alloy engines, giving the hatchbacks and estates top speeds around 95 mph (153 kmh).

ubaru Legacy

troduced in 1989 with a flatur engine (a type used by baru since 1980) and a sohisticated four-wheel drive stem, the Legacy has saloon or state bodies. The 1.8- and 2-re engines gave good performance (the Turbo had a 137 mph/20 kmh top speed). Extensively designed, with 2- or 2.2-litre ngines, for 1994. The 1995 GX estate has twin sunroofs.

Suzuki Vitara

In 1988, Suzuki slipped the Vitara three-door off-roader into a market niche, and in 1991 introduced the long-wheelbase five-door estate car illustrated. The first model was available with hardtop or soft-top. Common engine is a 1.6-litre unit, the JLX SE having fuel injection and giving the estate a top speed of just over 90 mph (145 kmh).

Suzuki Cappucino

While it could be suggested that this sports two-seater draws inspiration from old mode such as the Austin-Healey Sprite, it is more truly one of the Japanese micro cars of the 1990 It has a technically advanced 657 cc three-cylinder engine, but the top speed is electronical limited to less than 90 mph (145 kmh). It looks fun, and is – if you don't want to carry muc luggage.

Suzuki Baleno

The 1995 Baleno marked Suzuki move away from small-car policy, towards th small/medium sector, whe there are many competito such as the Ford Escort. It listed in four-door saloon three-door hatchback form both with a 1.6-litre fue injection engine. Th claimed top speed is 1(mph (175 kmh).

Toyota Corolla *(below)*

The Japanese dealer-franchise system leads to model names with long lives: the Corolla name was first used from 1966, and with the seventh Corolla *(illustrated)*, sales reached 20 million in 1992. That could hardly be regarded as a record, in view of the many changes, but gave backing to the claim that Corolla is 'the world's favourite car'. The range includes saloons, hatchbacks, and estate cars, and from 1994 the diesel SRD Liftback. These bread-and-butter cars are rated good in all respects, outstanding in none.

Toyota MR2 *(bottom)*

When this successful mid-engined two-seat sports car appeared in 1984, it had angular lines that were superseded by this smoother and longer body style in 1989. At the same time, a 1.6-litre engine was replaced by a 2-litre unit, and top speed rose from 120 mph (192 kmh) to 134 mph (215 kmh). A 1994 version, the MR2 GT, was a little slower, but at least it was less expensive than the T-bar Coupé. In aspects such as handling, the MR2 has a great reputation.

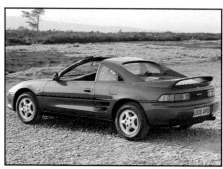

Toyota Camry

The Camry made its debut in 1983 as a medium saloon, Toyota's first model with a transverse engine driving the front wheels. A V6 was introduced with the third-series cars in 1989, and was carried through to this version, which has 2.2- or 3-litre V6 engines. These are refined power units, the larger giving a 130 mph (208 kmh) maximum speed.

Toyota Celica GT-Four

This is a car that has never been quite as fast as it looks, in the form illustrated or with its smooth 1995 lines. But it is quick from point to point, for its four-wheel drive gives above-average road holding and handling (and that justifies the association with the World Rally Championship winning car). The turbocharged 2-litre engine in this version gave a claimed 143 mph (230 kmh), whereas the 1995 version is a little slower.

Toyota Landcruiser

An imposing vehicle, the Landcruiser of the mid-1990s has lines that associate it with the first of the type, in 1981. It is best known in this long-wheelbase form, listed since 1987 and now rated a seven-seater (there is also a shorter Landcruiser II). It has a simple, rugged chassis and suspension This V has a 4.2-litre turbo diesel, which gives a top speed of just over 100 mph (160 kmh).

Toyota Previa

Compared with Landcruiser, this MPV is notable for its futuristic lines, but it is as practical and versatile. The engine is mid-mounted, angled under the floor, and this contributes to internal space (it will carry eight people). A GX designation, from late 1993, distinguishes the luxury version, which is

expensive among contemporary people carriers. It can reach 108 mph (173 kmh).

TVR Griffith

The small TVR compar
develops new models ve
quickly, to an establishe
pattern – a multitubular bac
bone chassis with outrigge
to carry fibreglass bodywor
(open and with two seats) ar
a large-capacity fron
mounted engine driving th
rear wheels. The Griffit
launched in 1992, is typical
all except the curving lines
its body. The 4-litre V8 giv
a supercar-class top spe
(over 160 mph/258 kmh). Th
cockpit gives an impressio
of luxury but, as ever, th
backbone is intrusive.

TVR V8S

The S was the mainstay
TVR production and sales
the early 1990s. Its lines hav
a familiar 'retro look', b
these are presumably le
slippery than the Griffith'
for speeds attained with th
same power unit are low
(146 mph/235 kmh ma
imum). Early versions – the
was launched in 1986 – ha
V6 engines of 2.8 and 2
litres (the car illustrated is
V8 S).

Vauxhall Astra

Astras have been familiar since 1980. The 3-/5-door hatchbacks in the third series came for 1992 and lasted into the second half of the decade, revised for 1995. It is also available in estate and cabriolet forms. The 2-litre GSi 16v Astra was a really hot hatch (135 mph/216 kmh), which gave way to the 1.8i. Engines are 1.4, 1.6 and 1.8 litres (a new 1.6 came in 1995), and a diesel.

Vauxhall Cavalier

The Vectra that took its place looked similar to the last Cavalier (*illustrated*). This version was launched in 1988, and built in saloon, hatchback and estate forms, with a range of engines from 1.4 to 2 litres. A 4wd 2-litre Cavalier came for 1988 and, with the 16-valve engine in 1989, this was a 137 mph (220 kmh) car.

Vauxhall Carlton

Almost a-quarter-of-a-million of this version of the Opel Rekord were sold, 1986–94, although it was overshadowed by the Senator for most of that time. A variety of 4-/6-cylinder engines was fitted. GSI in 1987 was a high-performance version, and a handful of Lotus Carltons were very fast cars, with twin-turbo 3.6-litre engines giving this four-seater saloon a 175 mph (280 kmh) capability.

Vauxhall Frontera

An adaptation of the Isuzu Mu (Amigo in the United States) enabled GM to enter th
European 'leisure-vehicle' market, using the name Frontera for versions with Vauxhall an
Opel badges. The two-door Sport (*illustrated*) has a removable rear section, while the T
is a five-door estate. The 2-litre Sport had a top speed approaching 100 mp
(160 kmh), while the 2.2-/2.4-litre versions were a little slower, and the 2.
litre turbo diesel reached 91 mph (147 kmh). In 1995 this diesel gav
way to an Isuzu 2.8-litre unit, while a new 2.2-litre
petrol engine meant that one Frontera variant could
reach 100 mph. These imposing vehicles have good road
characteristics, while rear suspension revisions in 1995
improved off-road capabilities.

Vauxhall Senator

In most respects the Carlton
with revised nose and tail,
well-equipped for the executive car market, and with good
handling and ride qualities,
the Senator was listed 1987–
93. Straight six engines of 2.5
and 3 litres were fitted, the
204 bhp version of the latter
giving 143 mph (229 kmh).
Most Senators were sold with
automatic transmission.

Vauxhall Corsa

If looks were everything, GM's small European model for the mid-1990s would conquer the continent. Interior space is good for a small car, but some of the engines, the transmission, and the handling and steering have all received critical reviews. The economy 1.2i reaches 83 mph (134 kmh), the 1.5-litre TD is a 104 mph (166 kmh) car, while the range-topping 1.6-litre GSi three door has a 118 mph (189 kmh) top speed.

Vauxhall Tigra

This engaging little sports coupé uses the Corsa chassis platform, its suspension in revised form, and its transmission, but it is much more than a 'hot Corsa'. It is nominally a 2+2 – realistically a two-seater with generous luggage space – with better handling than the Corsa, and a 1.4-litre engine that gives 111 mph (177 kmh) or a 1.6-litre unit (126 mph/201 kmh). Tigra has few rivals in its class.

Vauxhall Vectra

At first sight, the Vectra resembles the Cavalier it replaced in 1995, but Vauxhall claims that it is 'all new'. In important respects it is – wider and longer, and thus with more interior room, with a stiffer body shell and revised suspension to improve ride and handling, with a new steering layout to overcome Cavalier shortcomings in that area, with ABS a standard fitting, and so on. Engines range in capacity from 1.6 to 2 litres. There are options among equipment levels (but all Vectras have two front airbags) as Vauxhall fights hard for a major share of the important middle-market sector.

Volkswagen Golf

The Golf was an enormously successful replacement for the Beetle, and has always had front-mounted water-cooled engines driving the front wheels, as well as the sharp styling exemplified by this Mk II five-door hatchback. It had engines from 1 to 1.8 litres (giving 111 mph/178 kmh), and a diesel. The 4wd Syncro achieved a similar speed, and the GTI versions were faster, as are four of the 11 mid-1990s models.

Volkswagen Passat

Originally seen as another approach to VW's Beetle replacement problem, the Passat came in 1973 in saloon, hatchback, and estate forms, with Audi input. It was revised in 1980, took the form illustrated in 1988 (when the hatch was dropped) and was later restyled. From 1988 it has had transverse engines, and the 1.8-litre unit used in the Golf GTI gave it a 128 mph (205 kmh) top speed, with good ride and handling.

Vauxhall Calibra *(opposite)*

The Lotus Carlton was faster, but the Vauxhall performance-car image as the 1990s opened was to be found in the Calibra. The shapely four-seat coupé body was carried on a Cavalier chassis, and the car was launched in 1989 with a 2-litre engine, so there was 'more show than go'. That was put right in 1993, when a 2.5-litre V6 gave performance (a 143 mph/229 kmh maximum) to match looks. Critics may have found fault with handling, but had to agree that ground could be covered very rapidly in a Calibra.

Volkswagen Corrado

VW's first sports hatchback coupé has smooth lines, and an outstanding chassis and suspension. It was launched in 1989 with a 1.8-litre engine; in 1992 a version with the 2.8-litre VR6 was introduced, naturally driving the front wheels. With the 1.8-litre 16V engine it reached 126 mph (202 kmh), and, with the VR6, top speed is 146 mph (234 kmh). It is highly rated in most respects.

Volkswagen Polo

VW's first supermini, the Polo seemed a 'miniaturized three-door Golf' when it appeared for 1975; its slightly larger 1981 replacement lasted for thirteen years, with a facelift in 1990. The 1994 Polo shown has more rounded lines, with a good drag coefficient, and, for the first time in the Polo series, a five-door variant is offered. There are petrol engines – 1 litre (90 mph/144 kmh), 1.3 litres (97 mph/155 kmh), and 1.6 litres (107 mph/171 kmh), and a 1.9-litre diesel from 1995, with a five-speed manual gearbox and a four-speed automatic coming later in 1995.

Volvo 850

These larger Volvos have attracted wide praise as 'driver's cars', and combine sporting characteristics with cruising comfort. Even the GLT with a 2-litre five-cylinder engine can reach 120 mph (192 kmh), and the turbocharged 2.5-litre 'five' in the 850 T5 propels this estate car to more than 140 mph (125 kmh). The 850 SE illustrated is still faster, and the rare 850 T5-R has 'supercar' performance.

Volvo 400

The 400 series models are everyday cars, appreciated for sturdy reliability, while Volvo stresses the safety and economy virtues. Engines start with a 1.6-litre unit, but the 440 saloon and the 460 illustrated are also available with a 1.9-litre turbo diesel (giving a 110 mph/176 kmh top speed).

Volvo 480

The unusual lines of this sports coupé attracted much attention when it appeared in 1987, and it survived until 1995. It was the first front-wheel drive Volvo, launched with Renault 1.7-litre engines in three states of tune (including a turbo), and more recently with a 2-litre unit – in turbo form, this gives the 480 a 124 mph (198 kmh) top speed.

Volvo 700

This 760 estate car typified the big Volvo load carrier as the 1990s opened. Saloon and estate had been launched in 1984, were restyled in 1987, but, by Volvo standards, had fairly short lives. Engines were 2-/2.3-litre fours, a 2.8-litre V6, and a 2.4-litre diesel; with a turbocharged 2.3-litre engine, top speed was 120 mph (190 kmh).

Yugo Sana

The Zastava company badged its late cars 'Yugo'. The Sana was built 1989–92, and examples lingered in showrooms for some time after that. The mechanical elements were ex-Fiat, and aged, while ItalDesign styled the five-door hatchback body. A 1.4-litre engine gave up to 93 mph (149 kmh).

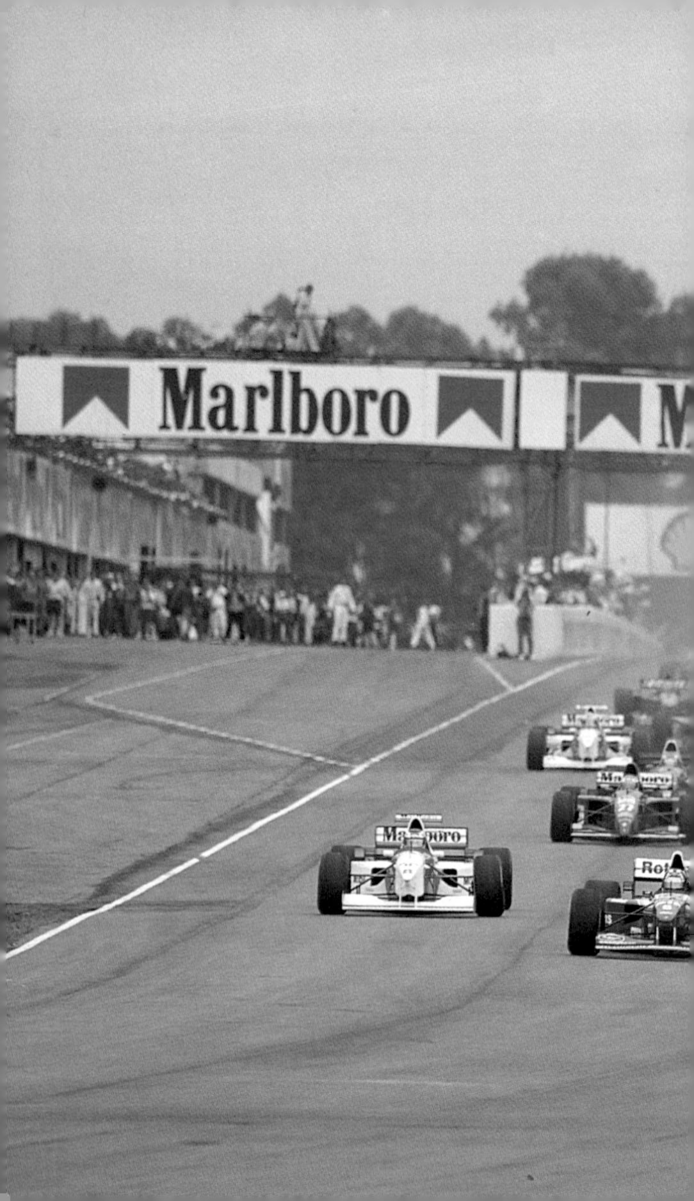
Marlboro

Grand Prix

World Champions

The two Formula 1 World Championships, for Drivers and Constructors (teams) are th twin pinnacles of motor sport, the drivers' series since 1950 and the constructors' serie since 1958 . The modern era dates back to the late 1950s, when front-engined cars becam outmoded. The basic layout of Grand Prix cars – and virtually every other successful racin car – since then has been similar to the Coopers that Jack Brabham drove to win his fir two titles, with the engine between cockpit and back axle. Unlike the simple Cooper however, modern racing cars are immensely sophisticated. The sharp contrasts are best seen in races for historic cars or in track demonstrations, while many of the classics can be seen at rest in museums.

A group of champions at Brands Hatch several years ago, with the one outstanding driver who won so many races, but never the world tit' Stirling Moss. From left to right, these great drivers are: Jackie Stewart; John Surtees; tl late Juan Manuel Fangio – to most enthusiasts, and other drivers, the greatest of them a Stirling Moss and the late Denny Hulme.

Mercedes-Benz W196

Fangio won the 1954–55 championships driving 'silver arrows', and Moss gained his first GP victory in one, in 1955. By the standards of the day, they were advanced and complex, and achieved a 75 per cent success rate, with nine GP victories.

Ferrari Dino 246

Phil Hill was the first American to win t World Championship, in 1961, and the la driver to win a GP in a front-engined car, 1960, in a 2.5-litre Ferrari Dino like this one is driving in the French GP. It was designat 'Dino' for Ferrari's son, '24' for engine capa ity, and '6' for the number of cylinders.

Jack Brabham

Jack Brabham was the first driver to win a Grand Prix in a car carrying his own name (in 1966). He is seen in the cockpit of a Brabham BT24 – 'B' for Brabham, 'T' for designer Ron Tauranac.

Cooper-Climax

Australian Brabham had already made history with his 1959–60 championships in Coopers such as this 2.5-litre T53 which he is racing in 1960.

Jim Clark

The late Jim Clark drove Lotus cars to twenty-five Grand Prix victories in only seventy-two starts, and was champion in 1963 and 1965.

Lotus 25

The Lotus 25 raced by Clark in 1963 looks skimpy, but it set a pattern for future cars with its monocoque chassis/body which was much stiffer and stronger than a tubular frame.

Ferrari 158

A sleek Ferrari 158 driven by John Surtees at Monaco in 1965. In Ferrari designations, 15 stood for engine capacity (1.5 litres) and 8 for the number of cylinders. Surtees won the world title with 156 and 158 Ferraris in 1964.

Graham Hill

The late Graham Hill was World Champion driving BRMs in 1962 and Lotus 49s in 1968. He won fourteen Grands Prix from 176 starts.

BRM P261

BRM's first Grand Prix victory came in 1959. In the 1960s it became a championship-winning team, with cars such as this 1.5-litre P261 driven at Monaco by Graham Hill.

Tyrrell 003

Ken Tyrrell's team enjoyed a golden period in the early 1970s, winning the Constructors' Championship in 1971–72, when its lead driver was Jackie Stewart (here in Tyrrell 003 in 1971).

Lotus 72

Lotus 72 introduced the 'wedge' body lines, as constructor Colin Chapman sought aerodynamic advantages. Team Lotus raced 72s from 1970 until 1975; this one is being driven at Brands Hatch by the 1970 Champion, Jochen Rindt.

Lotus 72D

Lotus development led to the 72D in 1972, still with pronounced 'wedge' lines. In six years Team Lotus won twenty GPs with the 72s. The driver is Fittipaldi.

McLaren M23

The McLaren M23 was another highly successful car, used 1973–76 and winning sixteen Grands Prix, driven by Hulme (here in 1973), Fittipaldi, and Hunt.

Emerson Fittipaldi

Emerson Fittipaldi was the first Brazilian to win the World Championship, in 1972 and 1974. He won fourteen GPs, then turned to Indy car racing in the 1980s. This photograph was taken in his first GP year, 1970.

Niki Lauda

Austrian Lauda started in 170 GPs, won twenty-five, and was World Champion in 1975 and 1977 with Ferrari, and in 1984 with McLaren. He survived a horrifying race accident and became a consultant to the Ferrari team in the 1990s.

James Hunt

The late James Hunt took the drivers' title 1976, after a dramatic season-long batt with Niki Lauda. Hunt started in ninety-tw GPs and won ten.

Mario Andretti

Mario Andretti (on the right) with his Lotu team mate Gunnar Nilsson. Andretti wo US midget title in 1964 and was still racin Indycars in 1994; his first GP was in 196 and he was fully committed to the worl series in 1975–81 (champion with Lotus i 1978). He started in 128 GPs and wo twelve.

Ferrari 312T

Niki Lauda in an elegant Ferrari 312T during his 1976 British GP battle with James Hunt. The 312s had powerful 12-cylinder engines and *trasversale* ('T') gearboxes, first seen in 1975 but outmoded in T4/T5 form in 1979.

Williams FW07

Frank Williams's team became a real force in racing with the FW07 in 1979; then Alan Jones drove the car in 'B' form to win the 1980 World Championship.

Lotus 79

In the Lotus 79, the airflow under the car was used to give 'ground effects' road-holding advantage. In this 1978 photograph, Andretti's 79 is followed by Lauda in a Brabham.

Renault RE30B

Renault started a power race when it introduced turbocharged engines in 1977. Before it withdrew in 1985, Renault turbo cars won fifteen GPs, but never the championship. This 1982 RE30B is driven by Alain Prost.

Brabham BT52

Brabham used BMW turbo engines from 1982, most successfully in the BT52 of 1983. Nelson Piquet is the driver in this 1983 Monaco shot, the year that he first won the world title.

McLaren MP4/8

After five years with Honda power units, McLaren used Ford V8s in the MP4/8 of 1993. Ayrton Senna – seen here in his 'home' Brazilian GP – took five races in these cars, bringing his total to forty-one in his first 158 races.

Nigel Mansell

Nigel Mansell (in cockpit) scored three of his thirty-one GP victories with Ferrari, the rest with the Williams team. His 1988–92 team mate, Riccardo Patrese (beside the cockpit) drove in a record 256 Grands Prix, and won six.

Mansell's Championship cars

The Williams FW14B (*left*) and the Lola T93/00 (*right*) gave Nigel Mansell back-to-back World Champion and PPG Indycar World Series titles in 1992 and 1993.

Championship Scoring

Since 1950 the World Championship scoring system has changed several times; now a driver can count all the points scored in a season. The first six in a Grand Prix score: 1st 10; 2nd 6; 3rd 4; 4th 3; 5th 2; 6th 1. Similar points are awarded to cars placed in the first six, both of a team's cars' scores counting towards the season's total.

Alain Prost

When Alain Prost retired at the end of 1993, he had scored fifty-one World Championship victories, and had been champion with McLaren in 1985–86 and 1989, and with Williams in 1993.

Williams FW15B

The Renault-powered Williams FW15B was an extremely advanced car – Prost drove it to seven victories in 1993 (here at Silverstone, on his way to his career fiftieth) while his team mate Damon Hill scored three wins.

Ayrton Senna

The late Ayrton Senna was the only past champion still competing as the 1994 season opened (he was champion in 1988, 1990, and 1991). Senna had started in 161 GPs, winning forty-one, and scored 614 points with Toleman, Lotus, and McLaren.

Michael Schumacher

First German driver to win the World Championship, Schumacher took the title from Damon Hill by the narrowest of margins – 1 point – in 1994. Through that sometime controversial season he drove Ford-engined Benetton B194s.

Index